The Circus Maximus and the Colosseum: The History of Ancient Rome's Most Famous Sports Venues
By Charles River Editors

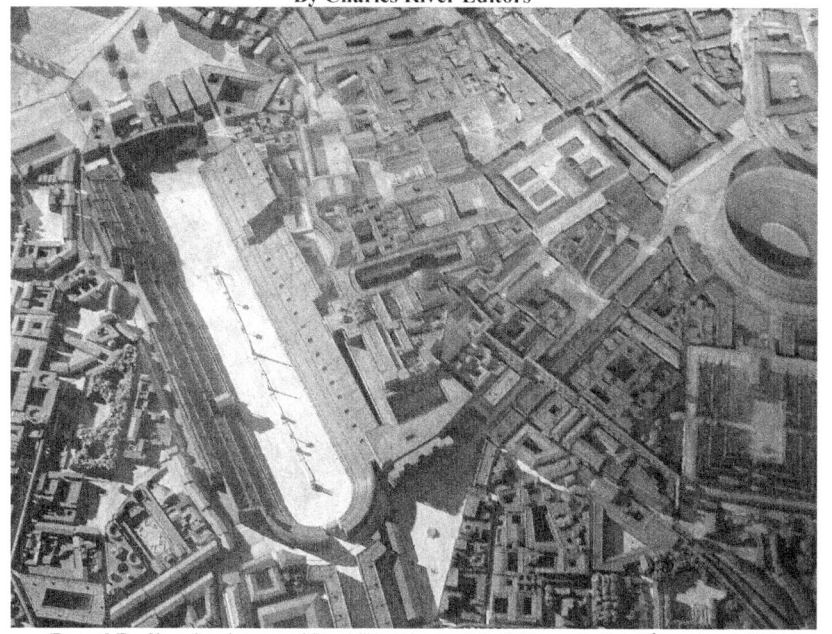

Pascal Radigue's picture of Paul Bigot's model of Rome in the 4th century CE

About Charles River Editors

Charles River Editors is a boutique digital publishing company, specializing in bringing history back to life with educational and engaging books on a wide range of topics. Keep up to date with our new and free offerings with this 5 second sign up on our weekly mailing list, and visit Our Kindle Author Page to see other recently published Kindle titles.

We make these books for you and always want to know our readers' opinions, so we encourage you to leave reviews and look forward to publishing new and exciting titles each week.

Introduction

A 20th century picture of the ruins of the Circus Maximus

The Circus Maximus

"Rome was a poem pressed into service as a city." In that short line, Anatole Broyard, a 20th century American writer, compactly captures the timeless and enchanting beauty that resides within the Eternal City of Rome. This tourist destination is often one of the highest ranked on bucket lists, for how could one not want to experience its marvelous ruins, mirror-like rivers, and spectacular stretches of aqueducts firsthand? As one sips on fine Italian wine on a terrace overlooking the grand remnants of the Colosseum, one can practically hear the roars of the battling gladiators and the raucous applause of the spectators. And as one strolls through the coarse, yet quaint cobblestone streets, one can almost hear the galloping horses and screeching wheels of chariots in the distance, and even feel the brush of the breeze as they charge past. It is difficult not to fall in love with a city so effortlessly nostalgic it verges on utopian.

The ambitious and fearless emperors that built the legendary Roman Empire from scratch, the broad-shouldered and bronzed gladiators with their iconic plume helmets and glinting swords, and elaborate parties attended by toga-wearing Romans fueled by alcohol, violence, orgies, and other godless acts all paint a picture of Roman life.

Indeed, many people are well-versed with these unique scenes of Roman history, and *Ben-Hur* helped popularize people's views of what went on at Rome's largest stadium. While the characters of Judah Ben-Hur and Messala were fictitious figures drawn from the imagination of novelist Lew Wallace, the setting of the rivals' classic confrontation, the fabled Circus Maximus, is very much real.

At the Circus Maximus, the guttural cheers of the spectators reverberated across the enormous open space, but their cries could hardly be heard over the rumble of the ground. On the ellipse-shaped track, 5 charioteers would skew their bodies and steer their magnificent vehicles around the curves. Gusts of sand and dirt flew up from the whizzing wheels and encircled the pounding hooves of the stunning stallions. Distracted personnel and guards dragging their feet were considered fair game. As one chariot careened to the side, preparing to collide with another chariot, a row of guards might have to try to duck out of the way in the nick of time. Some would be trampled by hooves.

Chariot races were dangerous for participants too. A charioteer could become disoriented and fail to position himself as his horses moved instinctively, sending his body catapulting forward out of the chariot. Needless to say, chariot racing in Rome was a nail-biting spectacle.

The Colosseum

18th century engraving of the Colosseum by Giovanni Battista Piranesi

"Let barbarous Memphis speak no more of the wonder of its pyramids, nor Assyrian toil boast of Babylon; nor let the soft Ionians be extolled for Trivia's temple; let the altar of many horns say nothing of Delos; nor let the Carians exalt to the skies with extravagant praises the Mausoleum poised on empty air. All labors yield to Caesar's Amphitheatre. Fame shall tell of one work instead of all." - Martial

When the Colosseum was built in the late 1st century A.D., the Romans, a people known for their architectural acumen, managed to amaze themselves. Martial, a Roman poet writing during the inauguration of the Colosseum, clearly believed the Colosseum was so grand a monument that it was even greater than the other Wonders of the Ancient World, which had been written about and visited endlessly by the Romans and Greeks in antiquity. Indeed, although the Wonders were wondrous to behold, the Colosseum was a spectacular achievement in architecture, something new and innovative, and therefore an amazing "Wonder" in its own way.

The Colosseum was designed to be both a symbol and show of strength by the famous Flavian emperors, most notably Vespasian and his sons Titus and Domitian. Vespasian had started the construction of the Colosseum shortly after becoming emperor in 69 A.D., but he died before he could present any spectacles in his giant amphitheatre. That honor went to his son Titus, who celebrated the inaugural opening in 80 A.D. with 100 days of games, despite the fact that the Colosseum was not completely finished. When his brother Domitian came to power in 81 A.D., he finished the amphitheatre, but not without making some changes to the overall design. By the time it was truly finished, the Colosseum stood about 150 feet tall, with the oval in the center stretching nearly two football fields long and over 500 feet across. The Colosseum is a large stadium even by today's standards, and its great size conveys the power of the empire as it dominates the landscape and towers over nearby buildings.

Nearly 2,000 years later, the Colosseum still amazes millions of people who come to visit it, and when asked to visualize a monument that represents the Roman Empire, many conjure up an image of the large amphitheater. As Keith Hopkins and Mary Beard put it, the Colosseum is "the most famous, and instantly recognizable, monument to have survived from the classical world." At the same time, the Colosseum also represents the Roman games and spectacles, particularly the gladiatorial combats that so many people today find both abhorrent yet fascinating. Given its massive size and the architectural ingenuity involved, the Colosseum played host to all sorts of games, including massive hunts of exotic animals and even sea battles.

The Circus Maximus and the Colosseum: The History of Ancient Rome's Most Famous Sports Venues explores the construction and activities that went on in both legendary places. Along with pictures depicting important people, places, and events, you will learn about the Circus Maximus like never before.

The Circus Maximus and the Colosseum: The History of Ancient Rome's Most Famous Sports Venues
About Charles River Editors
Introduction
   The Legendary Origins of the Circus Maximus
   The Origins of Chariot Racing
   A Tour Around the Circus Maximus
   The Charioteers and the Art of Racing
   Endless Entertainment
   Disaster and Decline
   Online Resources
   Bibliography
Free Books by Charles River Editors
Discounted Books by Charles River Editors

The Legendary Origins of the Circus Maximus

"It is not without good reason that gods and men chose this place to build our city: these hills with their pure air, this convenient river by which crops may be floated down...a sea handy to our needs, but far enough away to guard us from foreign fleets...All of these advantages shape this most favored of sites into a city destined for glory." – Livy, ancient Roman historian

Mere words are not enough to truly capture the brilliance of the Circus Maximus, but perhaps one particular legend sheds some light on its majesty. As it always is with age-old folklore, much of the story, down to the details of its conception, have been made hazy by time and the clashing versions presented by the innumerable writers that authored them. This is especially the case when it comes to the story of Romulus and Remus.

Some believe that the twins were conceived by Mars, the Roman god of war, and the mortal princess, Rhea Silvia, daughter of Numitor, the king of Alba Longa (a city by Alban Hill). Shortly before the disputed seed was injected into Rhea's womb, her uncle, Amulius, dethroned her father and seized his brother's crown. To safeguard his crown from those tempted to follow in his footsteps, he had all of Numitor's heirs executed.

Finally, the imprisoned Rhea was made a Vestal Virgin. These virgins were a syndicate of women whose patron mother was the goddess of the hearth and family, Vesta. Virgins not only vowed to refrain from all physical or carnal pleasures for life, they were tasked with fanning and maintaining the flames of a sacred fire. Thus, it would only be a matter of time before the authorities caught wind of the growing bulge in her belly. Exactly who it was that impregnated Rhea remains a matter of contention. As mentioned, some insisted that a frisky Mars, who was visiting Earth at the time, had seduced and bedded Rhea. Others speculated that Hercules might have been the mystery man. Then, there was Livy, who claimed that Rhea, having been violated by an unidentified mortal, was so ashamed of the rape that she cried "divine birth."

Whatever the case, Rhea, now a Vestal Virgin, was doomed, for virgins who failed to uphold their vows of celibacy were to be buried alive. After mulling it over, King Amulius, who wanted the cursed children gone but at the same time feared retaliation from the potentially paternal god, settled on middle ground. Rhea was thrown behind bars once more, and given an ultimatum that allowed her to choose the limited fates of her twins. They were to be buried alive, starved and exposed, or tossed into the Tiber River. Based on Amulius' logic, Alba Longa would be immune to the gods' wrath if the twins were to die in Mother Nature's hands.

Her hands tied, Rhea grudgingly selected the sentence with the highest probability of survival. She was allowed to name her sons, and after bidding them a quick goodbye, Amulius' servants ripped the wailing babies from her arms and stuffed them into a basket. Rather than hurl them into the tempestuous waters and leaving them to sink to the bottom, the consciences of the servants was said to have snuck up on them. Still, unwilling to prod another stick at the fully-woken and furious beast that was Amulius, the servants laid the basket delicately onto the river, watching helplessly as it drifted down the stream and out of sight.

Thankfully, the river god, Tibernus, had wised up to the attempted infanticide. He soothed the turbulent waters, and in time, the basket snagged onto a protruding branch by the foot of the Palatine. A female wolf known as the "*Lupercale,*" having sniffed their scent, crept out to the woods and discovered the basket. Intrigued, the *Lupercale* clamped her teeth around the handle and trotted back to its cave on the hill. She tended to the shaken, but otherwise unharmed twins, and nursed them with her milk as nearby woodpeckers collected berries amongst other treats for the hungry toddlers.

An ancient statue depicting the wolf and the twins

Months later, a shepherd and his wife, Faustulus and Acca Larentia, stumbled across the toddler twins, promptly fell in love with them, and brought them home to raise them as their own. The boys learned the ins and outs to the art of shepherding, and when they became teenagers, became sheep-herders themselves. One day, shepherds from Alba Longa wandered onto the Palatine Hill. The shepherds did not take kindly to the twins' kicking them out of their territory, and the alpha-male hostilities escalated to a full-blown scuffle. In the end, the boys failed to fend them off; even worse, they had captured Remus, and were now en route to see the king. The only silver lining was that Amulius, under the impression that the twins were long dead, failed to recognize the boys.

Romulus rounded up a gang of local shepherds as Remus presumably paced about in his cell, plotting his escape. In the stealth of the night, Romulus and his men marched towards Alba Longa and slunk into the tower where his brother was held captive. There, they subdued the guards and freed Remus. By the end of the chaotic rescue mission, King Amulius had fallen victim to Romulus' sword.

The twins may have ruled together if not for their cut-throat rivalry, which was just as strong as their brotherly bond. The citizens of Alba Longa offered them the crown, to which the twins politely rejected, for they thirsted for a challenge and hoped to create a powerful utopian city from scratch. Only, their grand visions did not line up, as Romulus fought to create a settlement on Palatine Hill, where the *Lupercale* had suckled them. The equally stubborn Remus, on the other hand, refused to budge from Aventine.

In the hopes of settling the squabble, the brothers agreed to an augury-off – whoever spotted more birds from the most sacred spots on their hills would be crowned the victor. Romulus claimed to have spotted 12 birds, whereas Remus counted only half that number. A smug Romulus puffed out his chest, but before he could do much else, Remus crossed his arms and declared himself the victor, arguing that he had seen his flock first. Unable to resolve the stalemate, the brothers parted ways and set out to establish their settlements on their respective hills, muttering bitterly along the way.

Romulus's first order of business was to order the construction of a wall and trench fencing in Palatine Hill. He eventually extended his walls to surround the Capitoline and Quirinal Hills, and later kings carried on the project and stretched the defensive borders across the Aventine and Caelian Hills, and under King Servius, to the Esquiline and Viminal Hills. Plutarch, Tacitus, and other ancient historians have described Romulus's fortifications as a simple, but effective "4-sided" set of walls, but not much else is known about them. These defensive walls proved fruitful when it came to staving off most potential attackers, but they only functioned as "physical boundaries." *Pomerium*, an Etruscan invention, which directly translates into "post wall," were so-called "formal boundaries" in the shape of marble slabs, or *"cippi,"* that identified these borders and the dimensions of the inner territories. The oldest known *pomerium* was supposedly installed by Romulus himself on the edge of Palatine Hill. These slabs multiplied as more sections were tacked onto the walls over the years. Anyone bearing weapons – even military officials – were turned away at the *pomerium*. Not even sovereigns were entitled to surpass the *pomerium* without a sanctioned escort.

Rather than let bygones be bygones and devote his efforts to building a comparable city of his own, Remus continued to harass his brother, and mocked his walls. On one occasion, Remus had been so keen on aggravating his twin that he leaped over the border in the middle of construction. Some say Remus lost his footing and slipped, snapping his neck upon his bad landing. In St. Jerome's version of events, a cackling Remus landed on his feet and frightened off the laborers, but he was later killed via a spade to his head by one of Romulus' radical admirers. However, most interpretations of the story have Romulus confronting his brother and throttling him to death on the spot. A remorseful Romulus buried his brother that same week with an extravagant send-off. With Remus out of the picture, Romulus christened his city "Rome," and his walls reintroduced as the "Square of Rome." 753 BCE has since been immortalized as the birth year of the Eternal City.

After Romulus had booted out the previous authorities, the hill's Arcadian residents were joined by a sudden spike of exiles, former criminals, escaped slaves, and other "dregs" of society seeking a new lease on life. With the male-to-female ratio severely unbalanced, the Romans on Palatine Hill had trouble spawning the next generation.

4 months after Rome was established, Romulus founded a festival devoted to Consus, the god of granary and good harvests (or the "equestrian Neptune"), which he dubbed the *"Consualia."* He had supposedly unearthed the altar of Consus while visiting the Circus Maximus, and was washed over by such a powerful godly spirit that it prompted him to create a day of sacrifices, public games, dramas, and other pageantry as an homage to the deity. Romulus' senators spread the word of the new festival, piquing the interests of the citizens around Rome.

On the day of the *Consualia*, tens of thousands of visitors from Crustumini, Antemnates, Caeninenses, and the Sabines of Old Latium teemed into the Circus, where the festival was to take place. As the colorful collection of citizens convened at the Circus were mostly rural folk, not one was prepared for the string of elaborate performances and thrilling games that Romulus had in store for them. Every eye in the stadium young and old was glued to the stage, the audience so captivated, they had slipped into an unshakable trance.

Romulus was seated in the front, dressed to impress in an ornate toga and a violet cloak ensemble. From the sidelines, his soldiers cracked their knuckles and cocked their heads from side to side, readying themselves for the signal with bated breath. At last, Romulus rose from his seat halfway through the festivities, folding his cloak and "throwing it over his body." All around the stadium, Romulus' men unsheathed their swords, and moved onto the next phase of the plan.

The crowd was said to have been so mesmerized by the chariot race that they failed to notice the armed soldiers slinking up the rafters. As the spectators continued to watch, the soldiers singled out the most beautiful Sabine maidens and heaved them over their shoulders, carrying them off the rafters and out of sight. The kicking and screaming of the women eventually broke the spell, but by then, a number of anywhere between 30 to 683 Sabine maidens had already been abducted. These young women became the unwilling wives and biological ovens of the Roman men in what is now remembered as the infamous "Rape of the Sabine Women." Some say that all this could have been avoided if it were not for the inexplicable, yet dangerously seductive allure of the Circus Maximus.

As gripping as the legend is, modern historians agree that it is mere legend. While the tale of a pair of feuding twins raised by wolves had all the elements of a bestseller, the origin story discussed above is most likely much closer to fact. Other historians believe that the term "*lupa*" might have been lost in translation, for the word also meant "prostitute." The same skeptics have suggested that, going against popular belief, the twins might have actually been fostered by a streetwalker, rather than a she-wolf. The *lupanar*, or cave in which the boys were raised in may have also been slang for a brothel. As a side note, other historians have also suggested that the city's name might have been derived from the archaic term for the Tiber River, which was "*Rumon.*"

Bearing all this in mind, archaeologists on Palatine Hill made a striking discovery in 2007. They unearthed what they believed might have been the said cave. Upon lowering their camera into a crevice on the roof of the "vaulted cavern" over 50 feet below ground, the bug-eyed scientists marveled at the rainbow of mosaics and dusty altars on their feed. They had found a shrine devoted to the *Lupercale,* leading some to argue that this more than hints at the truthfulness of the legend.

The Origins of Chariot Racing

"If you have overcome your inclination and not been overcome by it, you have reason to rejoice." – attributed to Roman playwright Titus Maccius Plautus

Long before the chariots were seen on the Roman racetracks, they were the world's very first locomotive artillery, and the "superweapon" of choice among Eurasian armies. Though the design of the war chariot seemed simple enough, its components were born centuries apart, delaying its creation.

First came early man's most pivotal invention – the wheel. Evidence suggests the first wheel, which was essentially a heavy slab of clay shaped into a flat disc, was created by the ancient Sumerians circa 3500 BCE. The Sumerians of Mesopotamia, who were situated in a strip of land nestled between the Euphrates and Tigris Rivers in what is now modern Iraq, were also some of the first people to institute a system of written language. It was by analyzing these texts that archaeologists today are able to decipher the Sumerians' studies on the wheel.

The first wheel functioned not as an instrument for transport, but as a potter's wheel. Potters slapped chunks of wet clay onto the wheel and spun the device around to give the jar, vase, or bowl its smooth edges and uniform shapes. In place of the wheel, Sumerians counted on handmade logs for conveyance. Objects or crates in need of relocation were propped up against 2 logs and rolled forward until the crate inevitably slipped off the poorly thought-out device.

When the Sumerians finally grew weary of the log method, they switched to "sledges," which were basically large sleds with curved edges and a smooth bottom that was slipped under the objects, supposedly making for easy gliding. Of course, the heavier the object, the more difficult it was to push or drag the sledge forward. The wheel might have been right in front of them, but it would take up to 3 more pre-wheel phases and another 3 centuries or so before the concept of using wheels as transportation dawned on them.

Next came the invention of the "composite bow," a C-shaped bow that is believed to have come into existence around 2800 BCE. Masterminded by the Egyptians, the bow was chiseled into shape with spears capped with beast horns. Bow-stringing was a 2-man job, and the string itself was fashioned out of sheep intestines. These new bows not only had improved aim, they could propel arrows nearly 1,000 feet. They quickly became a favorite of charioteers and cavalrymen.

Determining the origins of chariots, lightweight wooden vehicles drawn by one or more horses, has proved trickier. While some chroniclers link the first chariots to the ancient Egyptians, others believe that the chariot may have already been around more than 1,000 years before the rise of the New Kingdom. When Sir Leonard Woolley, an English archaeologist of the early 20th century, was in the midst of a dig in Iraq's Royal Cemetery of Ur, he dusted off a strange, 3-dimensional trapezoid made out of shell, lapis lazuli, and red limestone now known as the "Standard of Ur." The standard, which some speculate is the soundbox of some sort of musical instrument, featured scenes of war, and one of these scenes was of the "Mesopotamian war machines." These were 4-wheeled vehicles resembling wagons towed by a quartet of donkeys. In an effort to ensure that the art would not be abstract to its viewers, the artists included limp and deformed bodies under the hooves of the donkeys.

A picture of the Standard of Ur

In time, other civilizations adopted and enhanced these "proto-chariots" with their own alterations. Europeans, along with many others, fine-tuned the speed and design of the vehicle by eliminating 2 of its wheels. This marked the perfect transition into the chariot's final ingredient –

its horsepower. In 2500 BCE, horses were predominantly found in the "Eurasian steppe," a yawning piece of grassland that ran from Hungary to China. Along with the wild horses of the steppe – or "wasteland" – were clusters of wandering societies who relied on hunting and herding for sustenance. Contrary to popular belief, the settlers there herded these horses for food, as they did with sheep and cattle, rather than as transport or farm aids. They considered donkeys and other animals of the like much more suited for the task.

Today, donkeys are used as a last resort when it comes to deliveries over long distances, so the use of these animals might be baffling to some. Even more puzzling, not only was a horse only half of a donkey's price tag, the former is a far better candidate when it comes to navigating through steep, rugged, and other taxing landscapes. That said, scientists believe that the horses of ancient times were nothing like the strong and strapping creatures found today, and that a stallion well into its adulthood could trot no more than a handful of feet with a man on top of it before its knees buckled from the weight on its back. It was only much later, following the introduction of deliberate selective breeding, that horses bulked up in muscle and agility. Donkeys were gradually swapped out with horses between the years of 1800-1700 BCE.

Soon, rulers around the world, from Europe to China, had embraced the use of chariots in warfare, and these moving platforms of death became a common sight on the battlefield. Charioteers were not just chosen at random, either. In fact, they were talented soldiers put through hours upon hours of extensive training. While one charioteer piloted the vehicle, swerving away from incoming chariots and dodging the barrage of arrowheads, another armed soldier balanced himself on the platform behind him, firing arrow after arrow from composite bows and skewering opponents with javelins.

The most renowned of all the chariot battles was the Battle of Kadesh in 1294 BCE, which saw upwards of 100 Egyptian and Hittite chariots facing off in a legendary battle. The Egyptian chariots were modeled after the design mentioned above. The Hittites, on the other hand, opted for chariots with leather-coated bodies placed atop wooden frames. The frame was supported by a pair of spoked wheels modified to support the weight of 3 charioteers – the traditional driver and warrior – the latter equipped with distinctive spears and curved swords – accompanied by another wielding a massive iron shield.

An ancient depiction of Egyptian pharaoh Ramesses the Great using a composite bow and a chariot at the Battle of Kadesh

The Egyptian pharaoh Ramesses the Great attempted to quickly marshal his forces to Kadesh, but in the process he created a gap between the different divisions of his army in his haste. The trap was sprung by the Hittite forces just outside Kadesh, and the Ra division of his army was hit by an initial charge from Hittite chariots and routed before the battle had even properly begun. Surrounded and swiftly outnumbered, most of the Egyptian soldiers were killed in the ensuing chaos, and the Pharaoh himself was forced into retreating in order simply to survive. What is known of the rest of the battle is that Ramesses rallied his forces, fought on through the battlefield in order to evade capture and death, and managed to get away with only with a fraction of his troops. The majority of his army was slain on the field of battle that he left behind him.

The Battle of Kadesh was a devastating ambush, a strategic defeat, and the end of the pharaoh's campaign of conquest. The hopes Ramesses had held for claiming for Egypt both the city and territory around Kadesh were lost. But Ramesses had survived, and when he returned to Egypt, he set out to test the adage that history is written by the winners. Ramesses erected monuments, commissioned inscriptions and oversaw the decoration of reliefs all proclaiming the Battle of Kadesh as a major victory. His personal heroism and skill as a warrior were praised on inscriptions at such locations as Abydos, the Ramesseum, Karnak, Luxor and Abu Simbel. Ramesses had personal details inscribed that claimed, "No officer was with me, no charioteer, no soldier of the army, no shield-bearer..." and "I was before them like Seth in his monument. I found the mass of chariots in whose midst I was, scattering them before my horses..." In Luxor, it was written, "His majesty slaughtered the armed forces of the Hittites in their entirety, their great rulers and all their brothers ... their infantry and chariot troops fell prostrate, one on top of the other. His majesty killed them ... and they lay stretched out in front of their horses. But his majesty was alone, nobody accompanied him..." If the inscriptions were to be believed, the great warrior had singlehandedly ensured his own survival, even with all the odds stacked against him. Ramesses had successfully used propaganda inscribed onto the monuments and in the public places of Egypt to ensure that the people he ruled would deem him a victorious leader, even when he himself was faced with defeat.

Likewise, citizens hailed their soldiers as heroes for the most part, and the glorification of their "death machines" meant that the chariots were placed right on the pedestal with the brave souls risking their necks to protect their land. It would not be long before chariot "drag racing" emerged as a sport. Initially, it was incorporated into the underground scene, but in due time, it became part of mainstream culture, so much so that the acclaimed Greek poet Homer mentioned a chariot street race in *The Iliad*. 5 clan leaders – Eumelus, Antilochus, Merione, Menelaus, and Diomedes – were selected to compete in a chariot race in the countryside as a tribute to Achilles's fallen comrade, Patroclus. The rules were straightforward; once the charioteers took off from their starting points, they were to charge down a long and curved path until they reached their checkpoint, a tree stump ringed by a circle of white pebbles. They were then expected to steer their chariots around the trunk and rush back to the starting line. Diomedes, who was advised not to just care exquisitely for his stallions, but to hone his own skills as a driver beforehand, ultimately finished first, and he was awarded a cauldron and a female slave as his trophies.

It was more than likely that the Romans picked up on the tradition of chariot racing from their Greek neighbors, but either way, by the 1st century BCE, chariot racing had become one of the most popular sports in Rome. Indeed, it was popular enough that the seedy underbelly of society, smelling potential profits, began to tug at the strings from behind the scenes. Bookies began to crop up all over the land, orchestrating game after game and organizing betting syndicates for the illegal street races. As these were usually kept secret from the authorities, there was little to no regard for safety. Bystanders unaware that a race was taking place often received serious injuries from being struck by a passing chariot making a fiery turn, while an unlucky few with slower reflexes were squashed under the stampede of hooves.

In order to keep the hooliganism off the streets and the people content at the same time, authorities eventually decided to build an establishment designed to cater to the sport itself. This was none other than the Circus Maximus. Roman lore suggests that it was Romulus who had staged the first official chariot races, but modern chroniclers now believe that this entire story, as fascinating as it was, is no more than a myth, for the Circus had not yet existed during this timeframe.

To understand the vision, one must first crack a peek at the real visionary behind the Circus, an individual whose story was best summed up by Livy. Lucomo was born to a young Etruscan woman and a wealthy Greek runaway by the name of Demaratus. Demaratus had decamped from his motherland, where Lucomo was conceived, and settled in the Italian city of Tarquinii to flee from the stifling regime of Corinth's first tyrant, Cypselus. Little is known about the early years of Lucomo's life, but it is presumed that it must have been characterized by relative strain and volatility, what with his father's renegade status.

That said, even as refugees, Lucomo's family would have lived a rather comfortable life, for Demaratus had been a nobleman back in Corinth, and he had stowed away quite a bit of money for his family. In Tarquinii, Demaratus cooked up a new pottery business at his own, staffing his new enterprise by the port with expert potters from back home. Apart from bringing with him many of his Greek customs, which he shared with the Italians, he has also been credited with introducing writing and reading systems to the Etruscans.

When Demaratus died, Lucomo inherited all his wealth, for Demaratus had outlived his other son, Arruns. His money made him an instant magnet for single women, but he saw the value in connections, so he married Tanaquil, a priestess from a well-to-do Etruscan family. The gifted Tanaquil was just as ambitious – if not more – than her husband. She had grown accustomed to a certain level of luxury and societal prestige, and she urged Lucomo to think outside of the box and pursue greater things. While Lucomo was born there, being half-Greek, he was written off as a foreigner by the locals, so he found it difficult to penetrate public office there. After some convincing, Lucomo agreed to pack up their belongings and transfer to Rome, where money spoke louder than genealogy.

As the story goes, when the newlyweds strode into Rome on their great chariot, a bronze eagle swooped down from the skies, seemingly out of nowhere, and snatched up Lucomo's cap. Before he could curse the wretched bird for exposing his bald spot, the eagle returned and dropped the cap on his head once more before soaring off into the sky, vanishing as quickly as it came. The giddy Tanaquil took this as a "divine blessing" from the gods, believing they had chosen her husband as the king of Rome.

Hoping for a fresh start, Lucomo rebranded himself as "Lucius Tarquinis Priscus" in his new home. Having been educated by the most prestigious private tutors Tarquinii had to offer, Priscus made pals out of the Roman patricians, and from chumming it up with those in the upper echelons, he became close acquaintances with Ancus, the Roman king himself. King Ancus had treasured their friendship to such a degree that he appointed Priscus as his children's guardians.

When Ancus died of natural causes in 616 BCE, Priscus rolled up his sleeves with a glimmer in his eye. He sent the princes on a hunting trip, and while they were away, he rolled into town on his chariot to start his own campaign. The *Comitia Curiata*, or "Curiate Assembly," took a liking to him, and he managed to convince the Romans that he, rather than Ancus's youthful and inexperienced sons, was the man for the job.

As king, Priscus appointed up to 300 new senators and twice the number of knights. Following a terrible flood, he ordered the construction of the *Cloaca Maxima*, the first sewer system in Rome. To better protect his people, he refashioned Romulus's defensive barriers with stone, and he extended the walls so that it enclosed new territories. The Roman military was beefed up with new recruits and even the most seasoned veterans were trained some more. The army was presented with top-of-the-line weapons and armor with improved coverage. The cavalry was doubled, and the charioteers were provided with freshly-crafted chariots and more pre-battle training. His obsession with strengthening his troops would soon pay off.

King Priscus painted his first target on the Latins a little less than 3 decades into his reign. Under the king's orders, his men crept into the Latin town of Apiolae, pillaging all the homes and establishments and torching the whole place to the ground before hightailing it back to Rome, their sacks bulging with Latin booty. Around 3 years later, in 585 BCE, Sabine raiders stormed Rome, but they were promptly curbed by Priscus' vigilant guards and chased away by the cavalrymen. As the victor, Rome received the Latin-turned-Sabine town of Collatia. The Roman winning streak did not stop there, for the Latin cities of Ameriola, Cameria, Corniculum, Crustumerium, Ficulea, Nomentum, and Medullia swiftly joined the Roman repository.

September 13, 585 BCE marked the date of the glorious return of Priscus and his men to Rome, and only the most grandiose of homecoming celebrations would do this triumph justice. That day, Roman soldiers and horses trotted back into the city to the deafening cheers and fanfare from the mobs of people awaiting them by the city gates. Priscus entered the city in a gilded chariot with intricately carved vines detailing the sides of his vehicle, clad in a plum toga with golden palm leaves embroidered onto the silk. The crowds were shoved back to make room for a grand entrance accompanied by a procession of dancers, acrobats, and other sideshow performers. Each was dressed in a distinctive marvelous costume fabricated out of goatskin, their necks wreathed with flowers. Priscus and his men spent the rest of the day soaking it all in.

A Tour Around the Circus Maximus

"All of Rome is in the Circus today." – attributed to the 2nd century Roman poet Juvenal

After the victories, Priscus erected a temple as a tribute to the Roman god, Jupiter Optimus Maximus, on the Capitoline Hill with capital obtained from the Sabine and Latin hauls. But to the king, these gestures were not enough to demonstrate his gratitude to Jupiter for leading him to multiple victories. Since chariot racing was a particularly pressing issue at the time, Priscus, an avid charioteer himself, decided to knock out two birds with one stone. He authorized the construction of what would become known as the "Circo Massimo" (Circus Maximus), which directly translates into "Biggest Circus." Not only would this splendid stadium house the official chariot racing track of Rome, it would become the setting for what Priscus called the "Ludi Romani," a repertoire of religious games and performances held in honor of Jupiter.

The outlines of the Circus Maximus, or as it was known to the Roman public, the "Murcia," were traced around the valley sitting between the Palatine and Aventine Hills. The initial structure, made out of wood, was home to a track that was reminiscent of a slender horseshoe or bullet from an aerial point of view, but the dimensions of the stadium have been lost over time. While the "ovoid" shape of the circus was more appropriate for chariot races than gladiator matches, both types of entertainment could be found there.

There were said to have been no bleachers or seating sections in the crudely-built stadium for the first few years, which meant the first batch of spectators had to plop down on the grass on the hillsides. Some likely scaled cliffs for a better view of the action. Not wanting to be associated with the plebeians, a mismatching assortment of "raised seating," namely wooden benches, dotted the hillsides claimed by the Roman patricians. Hired muscles were later stationed in these deluxe areas to ward off the rest of the public. Many grumbled about the injustice of the seating placement, but almost every last one of them made do with what they had, for it was almost a crime to miss a second of the enthralling Circus action.

Dominion over the Circus would change hands as time progressed, well into the Roman Republic and Imperial Eras, and none of the first wooden structures lasted more than a couple of decades at most. It was only in the time of Julius Caesar, around 46 BCE, that the Circus' first "stable foundations" were planted into the ground, and the stadium's overall design finalized. In place of its timber exterior stood an immovable stone shell.

Gautier Poupeau's picture of an ancient bust of Caesar

Apart from the masonic makeover, Caesar extended the borders of the Circus until it ran about 1,800 feet in length and measured 350 feet across. He then created the first proper seating galleries for the masses, which ran along the 2 long sides and 1 curved bend of the open-air U-shape arena. These galleries, otherwise known as "fori," which were fixed atop a series of "stone arched vaults," are said to have been large enough to fit 150,000 eager viewers. Benches located on the topmost level were made of "volcanic tuff," the lower 2 tiers were assembled out of stone, and the rest of the seats in the middle were constructed out of sleek, dark wood. Seats made from "volcanic tuff," which was more or less the ancient Roman version of concrete, were later turned into marble.

One wing was reserved only for the Senators, Equites (a privileged class of Roman cavalry), high-ranking military personnel, as well as other patricians and their families. The cream of these crops were seated in their own private balconies positioned on the upper levels of the galleries, which was basically the ancient Roman take on the sky box.

The pulvinar, which was a special shrine built in the center of the uppermost tier, was later converted to an imperial balcony for the emperor and the royal family. This stately balcony, capped with a glinting golden roof, was adorned with carvings and vibrantly colored frescoes on all 4 sides. Here, the emperor could enjoy an unrivaled panoramic view of the games and festivities, all the while lounging on his comfortable cushioned chair as the servants posted on either side of him fanned him with palm leaves and dangled grapes over his mouth.

Due to the active presence of the untamed and bloodthirsty beasts in the Circus dungeons, strong iron railings that stood several feet in height were installed along the racetrack, as well as the galleries on all 3 sides of the stadium. Sadly, these railings were prone to rust and erosion. When Pompey the Great arranged a "terrifying spectacle" of an elephant battle, pitting 20 wild elephants against a group of trembling criminals, disaster struck. The masses, already unnerved after seeing about 500 lions killed before the elephant battle, suffered a mass wave of panic when the wounded elephants, "deploring their fate with a sort of wailing," smashed through the brittle railing in their agonized confusion.

A bust of Pompey

The missing hunks of the iron railings were quickly replaced, and the rest were repaired and strengthened with thicker iron poles. Caesar then added an *euripus*, or a moat, which was burrowed along the space between the racetrack and the seats. This moat, which was about 10 feet wide and 10 feet deep, served as an extra buffer, as it could trap unruly beasts. It would later be refilled and flattened over by Emperor Nero to create more room for spectators.

A bust of Nero

At its prime, the Circus Maximus was the largest sporting arena ever built – a record that allegedly still stands to this day. The astounding arena towered over its neighboring structures at 4 stories in height, stretching "half a Roman mile" on either side. More precisely, the Circus' whopping dimensions measured approximately 2,037 feet long, about 387 feet from one wall to another, and had a circumference of about 5,280 feet (one full mile). The maximum capacity of the Circus skyrocketed to 250,000, with some sources claiming it boasted enough seating for 375,000, though the latter is most likely an exaggerated figure that includes the spectators on the hillsides. More benches were added to the elevated seating galleries on every level, which made up 3 stories of the Circus' 4 floors alone.

Outside the venue was a "one-storied portico" furnished with a sprawling variety of 60 separate shops and commercial establishments. Pubs, brothels, launderettes, tailors, bakeries, restaurants, and dessert shops of varying sizes lined the portico. Tiny living spaces were also stacked on top of many of these establishments. Official betting stations and licensed pawn shops sat in the core of the Circus' shopping center, where spectators were free to place their wagers, or "sponsio," big or small. These were particularly fashionable, as wagers placed on religious games and events "done for virtue" were the only kinds of sponsio sanctioned by the Senate.

The corridors connecting the portico also featured latrines (communal toilets), hooked up to a nearby aqueduct that led to the Cloaca Maxima. Entrances to the arena could be accessed through the flights of stairs flanking each shop, which allowed spectators to come and go as they pleased without bumping into the knees of irritated viewers. Archaeologist Dr. Maria Letizia Buonfiglio raved about the commercial complex: "[This was] the biggest shopping mall in antiquity...a forerunner of modern football stadiums that pack in shops and restaurants to make money."

On top of the neat selection of shops was an array of temples built for different pagan gods, including the Temple of Ceres, a beautiful shrine embellished with handsome statues of terracotta and "gilt bronze." Yet another famous temple, which remained undiscovered until 1931, was a rather spacious building concealed 45 feet below ground. It is now believed to have been erected as an act of exaltation by a mystery cult that worshiped Mithra, the sun god and so-called "Pagan Christ."

By the time the archaeologists arrived, the temple's 5 rooms, which were connected by tunneled brick passages marked with arches, had already been stripped clean, save for a few artifacts here and there. One of the only artifacts that remained wholly intact and left in near-pristine condition was a clay frieze (a decorative tablet typically hung up on the wall) with an image of the god slitting a bull across the throat engraved into the panel.

Last, but certainly not least, was the stadium's racetrack, a bewitching beauty in its own league. Originally matted down with sand and gravel, the oval track ran about 1,772 feet long, and about 265 feet in girth, wide enough to fit up to 12 chariots side to side. A dozen carceres (starting gates) were posted along the opening of the U-shaped track, which were known as "ostia."

A bold white line drawn in chalk and lime was painted across the ground, right by the track's central divider. This served as the "alba linea," or "starting line." The moratores, or horse-groomers, were charged with keeping all these horses behind the white line. Above the alba linea were a pair of small statues sculpted in the form of Mercury, the patron god of trade, commerce, financial fortune, and the "fleet-footed messenger" of the Roman pantheon. The marble Mercury figurines were portrayed in their trademark winged caps, the chains connected to the closed gates of the carceres tethered around their outstretched arms.

Sitting right in the heart of the racetrack was the spina, a brick barrier that rose 6 feet off the ground and ran about 680 feet in length. The narrow boundary, which measured about 20 feet across, served as a divider that split the track in 2 so that charioteers could complete a lap. On either end of the spina was a trio of 20 foot tall cones dipped in gold known as "metae." Its base was garnished with bas reliefs that captured scenes from the greatest chariot races in ancient Roman history. The metae functioned as bumpers that absorbed the shock from potential collisions whenever the chariots made sharp turns.

Perched next to the metae were 2 stone columns topped with "crossbars of marble." Aligned on one of the crossbars was a sequence of 7 identical marble eggs studded with jewels and precious gems. On the opposite crossbar was a train of bronze dolphins. The eggs are believed to symbolize the Gemini twin gods of horses and esquites, Castor and Pollux, whereas the dolphins were selected in reverence to Neptune, the god of the seas.

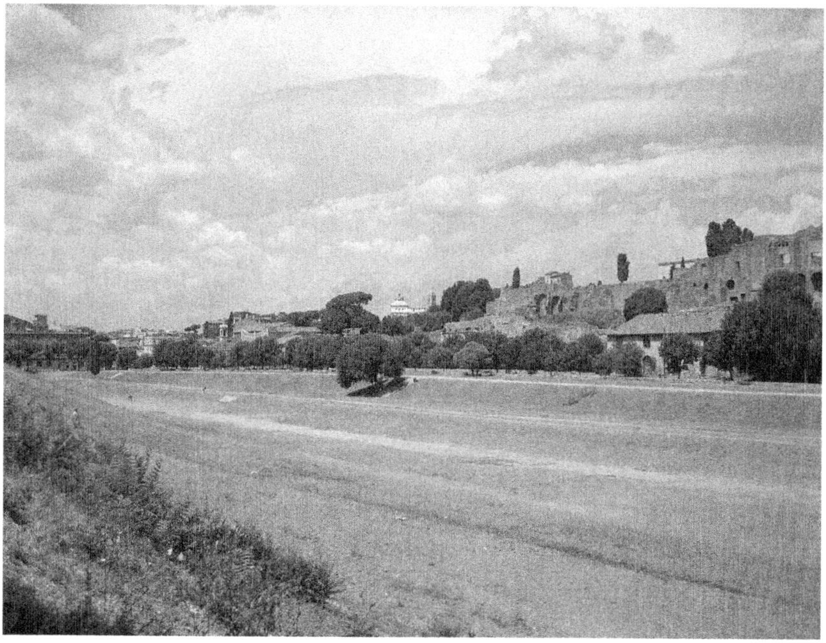

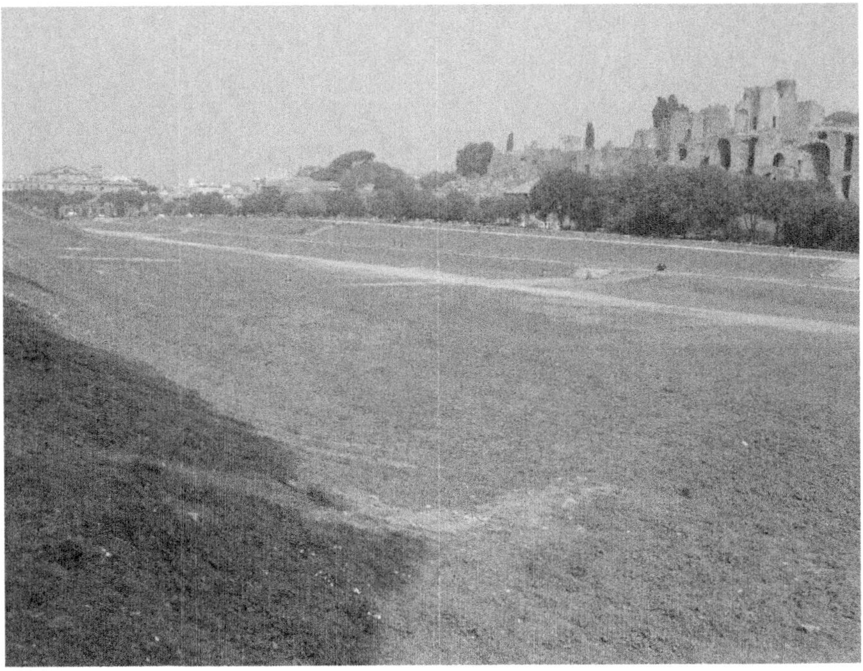

Pictures of the site today
The Charioteers and the Art of Racing
"I am Scorpus, the glory of the roaring Circus, the object of Rome's cheers and her short lived darling. The Fates, counting not my years but the number of my victories, judged me to be an old man." – epitaph of Scorpus, a legendary charioteer

Before the games of the Ludi Romani commenced, a spellbinding procession known as the "pompa" was first held. The pompa was spearheaded by the triumphator, which was the emperor. The triumphator would be decked out in his finest robes, his neck and fingers glittering with blinding jewels. Following the triumphator was the editor, or the host of the games, and a board of political luminaries and noblemen sponsoring the festivities.

A parade of each team of charioteers and horses; the competing gladiators both on horse and on foot; an assemblage of musicians, dancers, satirists, and other performers; and a line of priests sprinkling perfumed oils and waving incense sticks followed suit. Those on foot balanced tablet etchings and friezes of Jupiter, Castor and Pollux, and other gods and goddesses on their shoulders, whereas sculptures and other panels were carried by the priests and towed along in carriages. Silence swept over the crowd during the length of the pompa as a sign of respect to the deities, who would watch over their favorite teams and shower them with positive vibes and blessings.

The starting point of the pompa was usually situated at the crest of the Capitoline Hill, "the sacred mount of Rome." From the peak of the Capitoline, with the triumphator in his bigae or quadrigae (2 and 4 horsed chariots, respectively) leading the way, the paraders trekked through the Roman Forum, past the Sacred Way. They then turned back around and made the journey back to the Forum Boarium (a religious flatland that snaked through the spaces between the Aventine, Palatine, and Capitoline Hills), which touched borders with the carceres of the Circus Maximus.

Once the pompa had completed its rounds, the priests, with the aid of specially selected Roman consuls, transitioned to the performing of the sacred rites. A total of 12 (and later 24) chariot races interspersed by combative matches, dramas, and unique stage performances, collectively and aptly labeled the "spectacula," made up an average schedule at the Circus. At the end of each game, winners received symbolic palm branches and were crowned with laurel wreaths. These prizes were later upgraded to include cash prizes and other items of tremendous value.

The gameplay behind the millennia-old art of chariot racing is uncomplicated, and in many ways, remains similar to many modern sports today. Charioteers played in teams, or factions, recognizable by its team color – *albata* (white), *russata* (red), *prasina* (green), and *veneta* (blue). Colors were used in place of names so that spectators could easily distinguish the chariot of their team from great distances by fixating their eyes upon the colored blurs on the track, an endearing practice upheld by the Roman chariot racing community. Emperor Domitian later inaugurated 2 new teams, magenta and gold, but the public never took to these teams. Upon Domitian's death, the emperor's short-lived teams were retired.

Following the reading of the sacred rites, the competing charioteers drew numbers from a sack, then assumed their positions in the stalls behind their assigned carceres. Each faction was allowed a starter team, followed by 2 other spare teams in the next races, if they so desired. Separate races were held for bigae and quadrigae chariots; some lucky spectators caught the rare 10-horsed chariot race, too. An average of 4-6 chariots (and at times, up to 12) competed at one time.

With their fists fastened securely around their reins, the charioteers narrowed their eyes and peered out the slots of the spring-loaded gates, waiting for the signal. Before them stood the editor behind the glaring white line of the alba linea with a clean white cloth, known as a "mappa," clutched over his head. Once the mappa fluttered to the ground, the editor was escorted off the track at once. The gates flew open, and out came the charioteers, barreling out of their stalls, their faces scrunched up in concentration.

The spectators sprung to their feet, the stadium practically quaking from the roaring cheers and thunderous applause. All those present could keep track of the progress and the number of laps completed by paying attention to the dolphin and egg counters on the spina, an ingenious device masterminded by Agrippa, one of Emperor Augustus's most trusted confidantes. The 7 dolphins and eggs on either side of the spina indicated the total number of laps required to end the race. Each dolphin and egg was attached to a rope operated by a series of 7 levers below. Before the mappa-drop, each statuette was positioned to face north. Upon the completion of each lap, a lever was pulled on the opposite ends of the spina so that one dolphin and one egg was lowered. The remaining statuettes represented the number of remaining laps.

As it is with all sports and games, each charioteer harbored a treasury of knowledge packed with racing hacks and techniques imparted to them by their mentors. One of the most commonly-executed strategies is an age-old technique: the concept that slow and steady wins the race. Charioteers were advised to pace themselves and to watch their speed at the beginning of the race to avoid exhaustion on behalf of the stallions. Moreover, charioteers aimed to keep as close as they could to the *spina*, for this lessened the possibility of drifting and made for smoother turns around the divider. Since these chariots came sans steering wheels, racers maneuvered their vehicles by shifting their weight and leaning at the angle of their desired turn. Experienced charioteers looped their reins around their bodies like belts throughout the extent of the race, which was said to improve the accuracy of turns and served as a seatbelt of sorts. As a bonus, their free hands could be used to better support themselves on the unsteady platform, or to whip their steeds to accelerate their chariots.

Needless to say, the sport was one of the most dangerous and crash-happy of its kind to have ever existed. The technique of tying one's reins around themselves was marred by one disadvantage. While others could just dive out of their vehicles to avoid impending collisions, their only way out was to fish out the curved knife they had inserted into the holster around their waists and saw through the ropes. This was often a last resort, for charioteers were always determined to outshine their rivals with fancy tricks and showy gimmicks, not just to impress the crowd but because extra prizes might be in store for them. Still, knowing how to properly calibrate when it was appropriate to ditch one's chariot, and being fully aware of one's limits, were absolute musts. The crowds often lusted after the excitement and bloodshed, but during the worst pileups, sensitive audiences were known to rise from their seats and chastise the authorities for their refusal to stop the race. Others with hefty bets on the line demanded for the race to be stopped and started again, but their cries were almost always ignored.

In an age before steroids and other enhancements, physical or mechanical, charioteers relied on a nifty trick to improve their chances at winning. Licensed wheels followed the most basic design, consisting of wooden discs pieced together with adhesive derived from animal hides "that tighten[ed] upon drying, like clamps." However, some charioteers opted to install an iron rim on the right wheels of their chariots. Professor Bela Sandor of the University of Wisconsin at Madison illustrates the importance of these metal rims: "Adding the strip of...heat-shrunk...iron [onto the wood]...improved a charioteer's chances of winning a race to roughly 80%." Since most these races ran counterclockwise, "the right side tire works best if the turning is always leftward," allowing for neater, crisper turns.

One thing that set these ancient races apart from modern sports was the intentional lack of rules and regulations. There were no such things as red cards, timeouts, or penalties. On the contrary, competitors were encouraged to hurt their opponents, and the more creative they got, the better, since that only added to the nail-biting atmosphere of the extravaganza. The accounts of many historians tell the tales of sabotage conducted by immoral individuals who would do anything if it meant winning. Some even snuck into the stables and living quarters of the horses and charioteers and laced their food and drink with poison. During the race itself, charioteers were free to whack at their opponents with scourges and other lightweight weapons. Mortal enemies did what they could to yank their foes out of their chariots and toss them into the paths of incoming horses and wheels. They could stray from their lanes and zigzag their way through the track in the hopes of overtaking the chariots in front of them and disorientating the chariots behind them in one go. During races in which more than one chariot was allowed to compete for a faction, the charioteers collaborated with one another by sandwiching chariots between them and driving them right into the *spina*. Other chariots veiling clandestine alliances worked in teams to heighten the confusion on the track. These crashes were so anticipated by the audience that a term was coined for it: "naufragia," meaning "shipwrecks." The area by the metae of the spina was a naufragia hotspot. Early-bird spectators sought out and hogged the benches by the metae, for it was the most coveted of all the fori. Those seated in the very front were close enough to be drizzled by blood splatter, and they were given a premium view of many collisions.

Despite the immense amount of damage these chariots were known to cause, the racing vehicles themselves were rather light. In fact, chariots approved by the Circus weighed about 55-66 pounds. Its wheels were at least half the length of the chariot body itself, measuring about 2.1 feet across. As opposed to battle chariots, which were usually guarded by metal shells, those in the Circus were wooden and wrapped in leather. Additionally, unlike those used in war, the backless bodies of racing chariots provided almost no coverage, stopping short of the charioteer's groin.

Every horse enrolled in the Circus received a one-of-a-kind moniker of their own. Their names, breeds, achievements, and other relevant information would all be collected on papyrus scrolls by the moratores and other Circus staff. Favorite stallions of emperors and royals, as well as triumphant steeds, were often rewarded with prizes and treats catered to the animals' likes and dislikes.

The Circus games were open to all Romans and their Italian neighbors, regardless of class, and all entries were free of charge. Naturally, the spectator population, which divvied themselves up into fan clubs, overflowed with characters from all kinds of backgrounds drawn to the everyman sport, from kings and emperors to the lowest people in society. Chariot racing fans created nicknames to differentiate themselves from the other fans. For instance, fans of the Russata team proudly referred to themselves as the "great partisans of the Rusatta." Separate clubhouses were launched by fans of every faction, each member yoked to their teams and societies by an oath of fervent loyalty. In time, the most popular clubhouses, who lured dozens of powerful politicians and patricians to their fold, earned considerable political influence, and sponsored many a game.

Amidst the superstitious climate, manically diehard fans turned to pagan sorcery and witchcraft to curse opposing teams. A hex directed towards the Rusatta faction can be seen carved into a tablet discovered in the Circus excavation site: "Help me in the Circus on 8 November. Bind every limb, every sinew, the shoulders, the ankles, and the elbows of Olympus, Olympianus, Scortius, and Juvencus, the charioteers of the Red. Torment their minds, their intelligence, and their senses so that they may not know what they are doing, and knock out their eyes so that they may not see where they are going..."

The first charioteer to cross the finish line was greeted by the pulsing chants of the uproarious crowds. "Rejoice!" they ballyhooed as the winning chariot galloped around the stadium for its victory lap, the bloodied and battered charioteer beaming with pride. "Your Lords have conquered!"

Not everyone was amused by their antics. Celebrated statesman and author Pliny the Younger, for one, was far from it. He openly criticized extremist fans and condemned them for their reckless fanatical tendencies and immature behavior. "I am the more astonished that so many thousands of grown men should be possessed...with a childish passion to look at galloping horses...If, indeed, they were attracted by the swiftness of the horses or the skill of the men, one could account for this enthusiasm. But in fact it is a bit of cloth they favor, a bit of cloth that captivates them...if during the running the racers were to exchange colors, their partisans would change sides, and instantly forsake the very drivers and horses whom they were just before...clamorously saluting by name."

Riots and fracases were no stranger to the Circus. Not unlike many of the irritable sports fans of today, ancient Roman fans were often heavily inebriated, leading to poor judgment and short fuses. In one case recounted by the disgruntled Pliny, a fan was so overcome by emotion that he flung himself into the blazing wood cremating the body of a respected *Russata* charioteer named Felix.

In an effort to prevent brawls due to the bad blood between teams, the fori was split up into color-coded sections for fans of every faction. While this somewhat succeeded in lowering the amount of fan-on-fan violence, it also opened the gates to mob mentality. Some riots were triggered by losses or the death of a beloved charioteer, whereas some were said to have been spiked with "political undertones."

During the Roman Republic, teams were owned by private individuals who purchased these factions for princely sums. By the fall of the Republic, however, contract-based companies and firms made up the majority of team owners. In addition to financing and providing all the team's needs, these "owner-managers" hired scouts to scour the continent for the most talented horses and charioteers to add to their shining rosters. Few charioteers with solid careers remained in the same team. Team owners clung onto their star charioteers like koalas did trees, but bankrupt teams had no choice but to trade their favorites to keep themselves afloat.

The classic charioteer costume consisted of white, red, green, and blue tunics that hemmed just below the groin. Fasciae were 3 padded strips locked around the charioteer's torso and things, serving as his armor. Drivers were armed with a falx – the term for a curved knife – at all times so they could whip it out in the event of an emergency. Those looking to take out their rivals carried extra scourges and blunt weapons with them.

Some wore leather or iron helmets with various designs. Others were dome-shaped and fit snugly around the charioteer's head, either plain or with wings attached on both sides. Then, there were those that wore combat helmets with colored tassels and bright brushes along its center like mohawks. The dyed brushes on these helmets, known as "plumes," were placed atop helmets for more than just aesthetic purposes – the thick and coarse horse hairs were said to help cushion the blows from the weapons of crooked opponents.

It should come as no surprise that professional chariot racers went to all lengths to emerge as the victors, or "aurigae." In most cases, it was not just their livelihood but their freedom on the line. The bulk of the Circus' charioteers were slaves who pooled their winnings together to purchase their dignities back. Freed charioteers (liberti) at the top of their games could then demand higher compensation, and if their faction owners rebuffed them, they could easily fish for opportunities elsewhere. Those who scored more than 1,000 wins received not just the unwavering admiration and devotion of fans, but the honorable title of "millarius."

Many charioteers reached celebrity status not for their skills or the number of wins under their belts, but for simply surviving the track. The highly aggressive and often deadly sport claimed countless lives, the majority of them just shy of their 23rd birthdays. Even so, the young men who perished on the track could have completed hundreds of races by then, for most charioteers began their careers at age 18. The best charioteers – whether dead or retired – to have ever graced the tracks of the Circus were immortalized on stone monuments, some of them placed on top of their graves and others put on display at the Circus. Their career highlights and statistics – including their wins, the total amount of prize money earned, race settings, and their favorite horses – were inscribed on the plaques mounted onto these monuments.

Acquiring such fame was a double-edged sword on its own. While they were often lavished with praises and gifts from their fans and well-wishers, they had just as many jealous rivals and fans who would stop at nothing to tear them, or at least their reputation, apart. Detractors who could not wrap their minds around a charioteer's consecutive wins tagged them as evil sorcerers and magicians. One charioteer and his son accused of safeguarding the charioteer's win via the "black arts" were both sentenced to burn at the stakes for their crimes.

These feisty fan clubs were not confined to just the charioteers but extended to their steeds. After all, the horses played an equal if not more valuable role in the outcome of the race.

Longtime gamblers took team statistics under consideration, but they kept their eyes riveted on all lead horses. Master betters knew to avoid new horses, especially those that appeared skittish or easily spooked.

Audience favorites were often burly stallions who remained relatively motionless in their stalls. Well-groomed stallions with scintillating coats of freshly-washed fur and few scars and scratches were other signs of a choice horse. These signs indicated that they were well taken care of, and thus happier, but also that they had been in more than a few dicey races and knew what to expect. Some of the best stallions even had their own curses and jinxes conjured up for them. Conversely, there were those who had life-sized statues modeled after them and erected in their names.

The most venerated of all the Circus superstars was a man named Gaius Appuleius Diocles, one of the most remarkable rags-to-riches successes the world has ever known. Having been born into slavery, Diocles was barely literate, but his affinity with horses and chariots was one like no other. By the end of his 24-year career, he had won 1,462 matches out of 4,257, and he had amassed a jaw-dropping 35,863,120 sestertii in total. Not only was this supposedly enough to supply all of Rome with grain for a year, he could even buy up the entire Roman army on a whim if he so fancied. Today, his net worth amounts to about $15 billion USD, effectively making him the world's first sports billionaire and the richest athlete in history.

A sestertius of Trajan depicting the Circus Maximus

While the number of his wins was easily trumped by the records of Scorpus, who won 2,048, and Pompeius Musclosus, who won 3,559, Diocles's earnings were untouchable. All the more impressive, Diocles emerged from well over 4,000 races with no lasting injuries, ultimately dying peacefully in his sleep after spending the last years of his retirement curled up in the lap of luxury.

For his part, Scorpus was said to have been so idolized by his fans that they chucked satchels of gold at his feet at the end of every victorious race. He, too, was raised a slave, but he did not remain one for long, for he would be crowned with a laurel wreath over 2,000 times. Not only did his wins outrank that of Diocles, he had racked up all those triumphs in less than a decade. Regrettably, his promising career came skidding to a halt when he crashed into the metae and was thrown off his chariot, his body going limp under the unforgiving sea of hooves and wheels. He bled out from his internal injuries on the spot, aged 26. One of the witnesses, the poet Marshal, mourned the tragic accident: "Oh! Sad misfortune...that you, Scorpus, should be cut off in the flower of your youth...but O why should your own race have been so speedily run?"

Endless Entertainment

"You will remain sullied with the guilt of your fathers, Roman, until you have rebuilt the temples and restore all the ruined sanctuaries with their dark images of the gods, befouled with smoke." – Horace, Roman lyric poet of the 1st century BCE

While the Circus Maximus is most synonymous with chariot racing, the venue hosted more than just chariot races. In fact, the chariot races constituted only one side of the multifaceted gem that was the Ludi Romani (also known as the Ludi Magni). What was more, the Circus was home to a slew of other festivals showcasing their own unique productions.

The festival of Cerealia was only one of the many celebrations that elected to use the Circus as its venue. Held for a total of 8 days in mid-April, hundreds of thousands gathered there to salute Ceres, the Roman goddess of agriculture and fertility. Roman plebeians in particular flocked to Ceres in droves.

The main attraction of the Cerealia was the Ludi Ceriales, or the "Games of Ceres," which were scheduled for the 19th of the month, on the feast day of the goddess. In contrast to the Ludi Romani, organizers arranged pure horse races, rather than chariot matches. In 175 BCE, the Cerealia absorbed the customs of the Ludi Scaenici, and added a theatrical component to their docket.

The satires and improvised routines brought the spectators to their seats, but it was the elaborate tragedies and comedies that swayed them into staying. These dramas featured stereotypical characters that the audience grew to love, such as the adulescens, the dopey, lovesick bachelors; the leno, which were pimps and slave dealers; the miles gloriosis, the rough, no-nonsense military types; and the matrona, the nagging mothers and wives. Ovid described one of the most memorable scenes in one of the tragedies performed at the Cerealis, which involved a company of women in lace-white costumes fluttering around the oval of the Circus track with their flickering torches raised high. This was said to signify Ceres's quest to find her daughter, Prosperpina, who had been kidnapped by Pluto and held hostage in the Underworld. Ceres plunged into the Underworld in an attempt to fetch her daughter, but to her dismay, she discovered that Prosperpina was now perpetually cursed to spend every 6 months of the year in Hell for the rest of her life. The devastated Ceres was so heartbroken that the world seemed to freeze over without her daughter by her side, which in effect, gave the world the seasons of autumn and winter.

By the latter half of the 4th century, a play dramatizing the notorious Rape of the Sabine Women had become one of the most frequently performed plays in the Circus Maximus, reeling in morbid audiences with its "lewd and vulgar" subject matter.

Another Circus amusement was its boxing matches, popularized by Augustus. Suetonius shed light on the famous emperor's obsession with physical combat in his biography of Augustus: "His chief delight was to watch boxing, particularly when the fighters were Italians," explained Suetonius. "– and not merely professional bouts, in which he used to pit Italians against Greeks, but slogging matches between untrained roughs in narrow city alleys..."

Though these were commonly referred to as "boxing matches," these fights were more of wrestling and boxing hybrids. The Romans had a word for it – the Pankration, or "with all one's might and force." These fights were overseen by a referee, but that was about all that they had in common with their present day counterparts. There were no set rounds, nor were these matches timed. There were no old school versions of boxing gloves, either. All the sport entailed was 2 nude men tossing and turning around the floor in a tangled knot, trying to subdue the other. Spectators watched, sometimes for over an hour as the pair grappled with one another until one of them finally raised his index finger, conceding defeat. Like most ancient Roman sports, there were few to no rules. The only prohibitions were attacking below the belt or gouging out the eyes of one's opponent. These boxing matches were said to have been so brutal that many left the ring permanently disfigured. These were the lucky ones, for some never left the ring at all.

Even more engrossing were the gladiator battles of the Circus Maximus, which was perhaps the second biggest reason for the regularly packed seating galleries in the arena. This extremely vintage art form of armored sword dueling was one of the oldest Roman sports in existence, and like chariot racing, it found many partisans in the patrician class. Starting from as early as the 1st century BCE, specific schools were set up to coach gladiators, and other institutions were established to hone the skills of existing professionals. Many of the first gladiators were also slaves, and similar to charioteers, they could save up for their freedom if they truly worked at it and succeeded in their fields. Also like the charioteers, gladiators were often lauded as heroes, or "primus palus," and boasted their own fan clubs. Some of the biggest names were even classed as sex symbols. As opposed to most ancient Roman sports, there were said to have been quite a few female gladiators, but even less were treated as actual sportsmen. Rather, female gladiators were often signed on as "comedic" acts and made to face off with midgets.

Politicians and nobles such as Caesar and Cicero were known to have been the proud owners of several household names in the gladiator world, as they were considered wise investments. Gladiators were always in high demand, particularly so at the Circus Maximus, and they were always guaranteed to draw a crowd, no matter the venue. The popularity of the sport steadily soared over the years, and in time, the number of free men readily trying out for a shot at glory outmatched that of the slave gladiators. Despite the obvious hazards the sport entailed, the adrenaline, coupled with the fame and the earth-shattering cheers from the stands, was a siren song they could not resist.

The Circus Maximus also held contests for all sorts of mighty beasts from faraway lands, which were made to square off with each other in another ludi spectacle known as the "venationes." On special occasions, gladiators or condemned criminals were thrust before these feral beasts, which could be anything from a petrifying panther to a horrifying hippopotamus. When they were not in the ring, the animals were kept chained up in pitch-black pits and dungeons.

While the prized stallions of the Circus were given the royal treatment, the same could not be said for the Circus beasts. The bestiarii, or animal handlers, were instructed to force-feed would-be herbivores chunks of meat, and skimp out on the rations so that the animals would grow aggravated and fight each other for their share. Before the games began, the bestiarii prodded at them with sticks and riled them up in other ways to provoke them, making for a better show.

On a lighter note, not all those who visited the Circus were there for the guts and gore. Young men looking for dates were known to prowl the arena for girls, many of them lifting tips straight out of Ovid's *The Art of Love*, which contained an entire passage on how to pick up women at the Circus. As Ovid put it, "in the crowds at the track, opportunity waits." With that in mind, many of these tips would certainly be considered sexual harassment today. An excerpt from the passage stated, "There is no need for a code of finger-signals or nodding. Sit as close as you like; no one will stop you at all. In fact, you will have to sit close – that's one of the rules, at a race track. Whether she likes it or not, contact is part of the game..." Another gem egged the readers on: "If her cloak hangs low, and the ground is getting dirty, gather it up with care, lift it a little, so! Maybe by way of reward, and not without her indulgence, you'll be able to see ankle or possibly knee."

Disaster and Decline

To say that the Circus Maximus was a sight to behold in its heyday would be a bold understatement. It was the epitome of the new wealth the ever-growing city of Rome was now swimming in, given its spacious facilities, elegantly designed structure, top-drawer equipment, priceless treasures, and the overall opulence practically exuding from the stupendous stadium. Unfortunately, all its resplendence could not save it from the disaster constantly waiting around the bend, a problem that overambitious structures built in primitive times could never escape. Ironically, the harbinger of the Circus disasters, in hindsight, could have very well been avoided if proper precautions were enforced. A fierce fire, which presumably originated from one of the eateries in the Circus portico, consumed almost all of the wooden bleachers. It was only then that the succeeding Roman rulers learned from their predecessor's errors and rebuilt the Circus so that most of it was fortified with stone.

Soon after Emperor Augustus had the Imperial Box constructed, he installed a giant 86 foot tall obelisk in the center of the spina. The obelisk, a slim stone pillar that somewhat resembled a taper candle, was built out of pink aswan granite and transported all the way from the ancient Egyptian city of Heliopolis. Many historians are now convinced that this sacred monument, which was assembled for Ra, the Egyptian sun god, was something of a good luck charm that intended to aid the sportsmen and performers at the Circus and keep the venue safe from the wrath of the gods. The obelisk may have also served as a giant sundial for the city, but the obelisk did little to help matters, for disaster persisted.

The obelisk

A sestertius depicting the Circus Maximus and the obelisk

Ironically, one of the most famous fires of the Circus – and in all of Roman history – occurred under the reign of one of the most passionate chariot racing fans. Emperor Nero was said to have been so infatuated with the sport that he often barged into chariot races uninvited. On one occasion, he showed up to a quadrigae race with a 10-horse chariot, but of course, even with what little rules there were, not one of them applied to him. Even when the obese emperor bumbled his way through the tracks, failing to completing even 2 of the 7 laps, he was crowned the winner.

In mid-July of 64 CE, a terrible fire erupted in the shopping center close to the Circus Maximus, and despite the firefighters' best efforts, the flames raged on for 6 days, eventually spreading to the slums. The dry, wooden buildings and harsh gusts of winds acted as its accelerant, and by the time the flames were contained, nearly 67% of the city was nothing but rubble and debris, large chunks of which hid dozens of corpses. Among the casualties of the fire were the Temple of Jupiter Stator, the Atrium Vestae, and hundreds of Romans, while thousands wept over the scorched remnants of their homes. Given its location, the fire tore through the Circus, swallowing the fori, spina, and every last one of the 60-something shops in its merciless flames.

What appears most likely is that the fire was an accident, likely caused by flammable materials near the Circus Maximus. Indeed, blazes of such kind were common until the 19th century, which had no shortage of overcrowded cities with wooden houses closely packed together, lit and heated by open flames and with no organized official fire brigades. Rome would suffer two more major fires in the next 15 years.

However, the grapevines were soon abuzz with rumors that Emperor Nero was the culprit. Many speculated that it was his desperate attempt at snaking around the stifling senate so that he could renovate Rome as he so pleased. Though there was plenty of evidence to suggest that Nero was more than 35 miles away when the fire began, he opted for the easy way out by pointing his finger at the Christians. The secretive sect, which still boasted only small numbers but was fast growing in popularity, was viewed with suspicion and even hatred, as the Jews also were, by much of the Roman Empire. The main reason for this dislike was simple: the other pagan polytheistic traditions which flourished side by side throughout the empire might advocate the superiority of their own particular gods but, unlike the Christians, would not deny the existence of others. Christians flat-out believed that theirs was the only true God, and were not afraid to say so. Consequently, they were highly unpopular.

Nero capitalized on that unpopularity by accusing Christians of being responsible for the blaze, though it does not appear as though any motive was ever ascribed to them. Several were seized and, after being tortured, confessed (it is unclear whether they confessed to being Christians, or to the arson itself, but most sources are in accord in saying that they confessed *because* they were tortured). Scores of Christians were martyred, some draped in the skins of wild animals and then torn apart by dogs in the arena, others crucified in a mockery of Jesus's martyrdom, and still more were burned alive, nightly, to serve as illumination for Nero's garden banquets. The first institutionalized persecution of the Christians in the history of the Roman Empire (but not the last) had begun.

At the same time, Nero took advantage of the fire to quickly build the *Domus Aurea*, the extraordinary imperial residence on the Esquiline, which ran from the Oppian peak to the Palatine. Historian Eric Varner concisely sums up the grumbling public's sentiments: "They would have been happy if Nero had built the *Domus Aurea* out in the country, but to do it here in the city really was an extraordinary kind of statement."

As it turned out, the disasters that dogged the Circus could not be blamed for the stadium's eventual decline. Towards the last years of the 200s, Emperor Probus organized one of the most striking beast hunts the Circus had ever seen. Dozens of trees, shrubs, and a vast array of plants were uprooted and arranged in the back of a makeshift platform, and mounds of earth and sand were smoothed out across the floor. Amidst this splendid and highly realistic backdrop, over 1,000 stags, sheep, boars, and grass-eating creatures were paraded across the stage. When the signal was given, the spectators rushed forth and seized as many beasts as they could in a chaotic free-for-all.

When Christianity began to prevail with the help of Constantine the Great in the next century, interest in the pagan games began to peter out. As such, the Circus was rendered virtually useless. The Christian public was put off by chariot races, which the papacy often associated with sorcery and black magic. In fact, Christian authorities were so hell-bent on burying the sport that they ordered all charioteers to "publicly renounce their professions" if they wanted in on the religion. The final chariot race of the Circus Maximus, which was held in 549 by Totila, the King of the Ostrogoths, barely managed to fill half the stadium, a sight that would have made the greatest Circus lovers roll over in their graves. By the late 6th century, the Circus was officially defunct.

By the Renaissance, the site of the Circus Maximus had become nothing more than an infertile, swampy plot of land. To rectify this, Pope Sixtus V ordered for most of the site to be buried several feet underground, with new fertile earth paved over it. A considerable stretch of these ruins has since been excavated and now stand on display at the original site. Though the obelisks and *spina* are now long gone, what is left of the legendary oval track has been converted to a small, charming park, visited by thousands of locals and tourists daily. It has also hosted several concerts and public celebrations, such as the funeral of Pope John Paul II. Though it might have been centuries since an actual chariot has rolled across the racetrack, it is clear that the locals are not willing to let this fabled place fade into the background just yet.

The Origins of the Colosseum

Even before it was built, the Colosseum was unique, based solely on its proposed location. Traditionally, amphitheatres were constructed on the edges of Roman cities, but the Colosseum was constructed where it presently stands within the heart of the city. Naturally, there was a reason why it was built where it was.

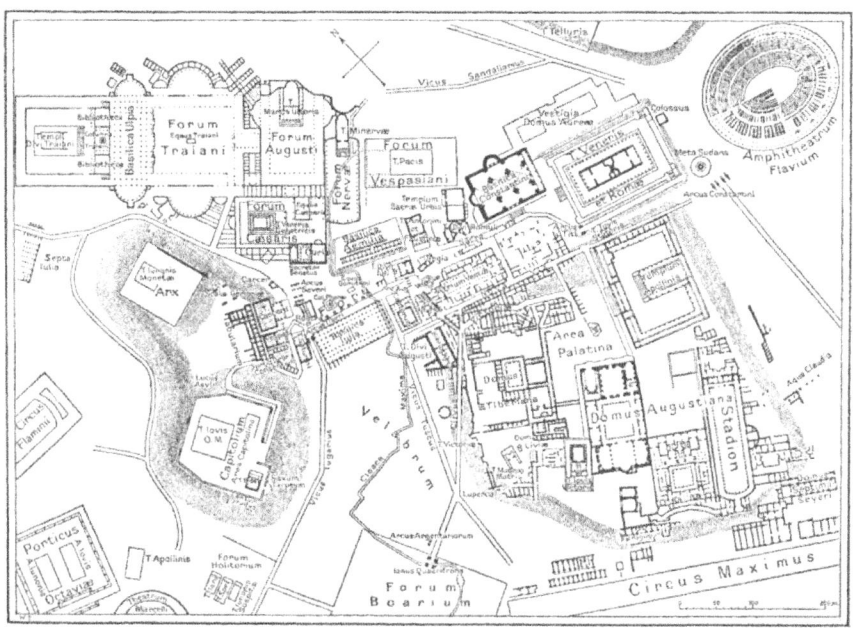

Map of Rome, with the Colosseum marked near the top right as the Amphitheatrum Flavium

The last Julio-Claudian emperor of Rome before the Flavians was Nero, who was notorious for his cruelty toward Christians and the popular misconception that he fiddled while Rome burned. It was during his reign in 64 A.D. that a fire razed a great majority of Rome, and one of the most important sections destroyed in the blaze was the area from the Palatine to the Esquiline Hill. This was previously private land, but Nero decided to confiscate this portion of the city and turn it into his own private imperial estate. Not surprisingly, the emperor spared no expense when constructing his own personal villa in the heart of Rome, and Suetonius, an early 2nd century biographer, described Nero's house in his biography of the emperor:

> "Nero built a palace stretching from the Palatine to the Esquiline, which was at first called the *Domus Transitoria*, but after it had burnt in the fire it was restored and was called the *Domus Aurea*. The following facts will serve to give some idea of its size and luxury. In its vestibulum there was a colossal statue of Nero 120 feet high; and so spacious was it that it had a portico a mile long. There was an artificial lake to represent the sea, and on its shores were buildings laid out as cities; and there were stretches of countryside, with fields and vineyards, pastures and woodlands, and among them were herds of domestic animals and all sorts of beasts. In other parts it was overlaid with gold and jewels and mother of pearl. There were dining halls whose ivory ceilings were set with pipes to sprinkle the guests with flowers and perfume. The main dining hall was circular and it revolved constantly day and night

like the universe. There were also sea water baths and baths of sulfur water. When Nero moved in, he only deigned to remark 'At last I can begin to live like a human being.'"[1]

Only a single wing of the "Golden House" survives today, because this section of the house was subsequently used as a substructure for the Baths of Trajan. On the walls of this wing are elaborate paintings that once influenced Renaissance painters, but the rest of the house was damaged by fire in AD 104 and subsequently removed.

Ruins of the Baths of Trajan

When Nero committed suicide in 68 A.D., the following year saw four men fight to become the next emperor of the Roman Empire, with Vespasian emerging victorious. As a successful general and experienced civil servant, he was accepted by the Roman people and senate, and it did not hurt that he also had the backing of some military commanders and senators. Another advantage Vespasian brought as emperor was that he already had two sons, which meant he had two heirs, an important fact for the Romans as they did not want to see another civil war too soon.

Despite his already existing popularity, Vespasian wanted to impress upon the Roman people his power, worth and beneficence as the first ruler of a new imperial dynasty, and to accomplish this, Vespasian and his sons wanted to discredit and distance themselves from the previous "bad" emperor Nero. Vespasian did this in a number of ways, including rebuilding a Temple of Jupiter and constructing a Temple of Peace, the latter of which was erected in order to celebrate his

---

[1] Suetonius, *Nero*.31, in Welch (2007) p149.

victory over the Jews in 71. This was an important triumph not only because it added to his reputation as a successful general but also because the spoils from this war filled the imperial coffers. As a result, when Vespasian spent money building monuments in Rome, it was not at the expense of the Roman people.[2]

Vespasian's greatest gift to the Roman people was an amphitheatre that would become known as the Colosseum, and his choice to build an amphitheatre where Nero's artificial lake was located was a carefully planned one. The artificial lake was on part of the land confiscated by Nero for his own private use, so by choosing this spot, Vespasian was essentially returning the land back to the Roman people. Thus, the Colosseum would not only become an entertainment facility for the city of Rome but also a political statement by the Flavians. It was a way for Vespasian to clearly distance himself from the wrongs Nero had committed against the Roman people, and it is evident that the Roman people recognized Vespasian's intentions, as Martial noted:

> "Where the starry Colossus sees the constellations at close range and lofty scaffolding rises in the middle of the road, once gleamed the odious halls of a cruel monarch, and in all Rome there stood a single house. Where rises before our eyes the august pile of the Amphitheatre, was once Nero's lake. Where we admire the warm baths [Baths of Titus], a speedy gift, a haughty tract of land had robbed the poor of their dwellings. Where the Claudian colonnade [substructures on the Temple of Divine Claudius] unfolds its widespread shade, was the outermost part of the palace's end. Rome has been restored to herself, and under your rule, Caesar, the pleasances that belonged to a master now belong to the people."[3]

The Colosseum also represented Vespasian's military victory over the Jews, as documented on an inscription believed to have once adorned the building. The inscription was on a block of stone that was reused in the 5th century to commemorate the restoration of the Colosseum, and even though the original bronze letters were missing, scholars noticed that underneath the 5th century inscription were holes from an earlier inscription. By measuring the distance between the holes, scholars were able to reconstruct what the original wording might have been. Reconstructed, this inscription read: 'The emperor Titus Caesar Vespasian Augustus had the new amphitheatre built from the profits of war." Whether this is accurate or just wishful thinking, the fact remains that the Colosseum was constructed in part to commemorate Vespasian's victory over the Jews.[4]

Despite Vespasian's attempts to erase the memory of Nero by constructing an amphitheatre for the people, the name of this structure still has links to that emperor. In antiquity, Vespasian's amphitheatre was more commonly referred to as "the Amphitheatre" or the "Hunting Theatre". By the Middle Ages the amphitheatre was referred to as the Colosseum, no doubt due at least in part to the sheer size of the structure, but another reason for this name was because of the Colossus, a colossal statue of Nero that stood nearby and had been originally placed in the vestibule of his Golden House. It is believed that this colossal statue continued to stand near the amphitheatre long after the Golden House was removed (albeit with the face made to look less like Nero), and the base for the statue was located near the Colosseum until at least the 1930's,

---

[2] Hopkins & Beard (2005) p.28.
[3] Martial, *Spectacles*.2, in Welch (2007) p.148.
[4] Welch (2007) p.160, Köhne & Ewigleben (2000) p.24 & Hopkins & Beard (2005) p.33.

when Mussolini had the area cleaned up in order to make his road. The exact date of the statue's removal remains uncertain, but either way, it's ironic that the modern name of Vespasian's amphitheatre actually refers in part to a statue of the emperor Nero, the man that Vespasian wanted the Roman people to forget when he constructed his monument.[5]

Designing and Building the Colosseum

"While stands the Coliseum, Rome shall stand; When falls the Coliseum, Rome shall fall; And when Rome falls - the World." – Lord Byron

The Colosseum was not the first amphitheatre to be built within the city of Rome. In fact, before its construction, whenever an aristocrat or emperor wanted to hold gladiatorial combats, a temporary wooden amphitheatre would be constructed and often dismantled after the show. There was a fear among Roman magistrates that people would continually gather and express their views if there was a permanent structure, and the Romans were also not overly enthusiastic about any permanent structure dedicated to pleasure, since that suggested extravagance and decadence, something many Romans wished to avoid.

Other than a temporary amphitheatre, it was common for spectacles to be held within the Forum, Circus Maximus, or any other building that had enough accommodating space. The problem with most of these facilities was that they were hardly suitable to hold large spectacles, and another major issue was that they did not possess satisfactory safety precautions when animals were displayed. Therefore, the construction of a permanent stone amphitheatre was a momentous occasion for the people, as it would not only be a place to enjoy spectacles but a forum where they could collectively vent their frustrations to the emperor.[6]

The design of an amphitheatre is commonly described as two theatres joined together back to back to form one large elliptical center surrounded by seats. But despite an understanding this general description, determining exactly how the Romans laid out the perimeter of the Colosseum is still somewhat of a mystery. Although the Colosseum appears to be a perfect ellipse, its shape is actually an ovoid, which is a polycentric curve, because it has more than one center. If the structure had been a true ellipse, then the inner wall of the arena would not have been parallel to the outer wall, and adjustments would have continually needed to be made in order to ensure that they were in fact parallel. How the Romans accomplished this is where the question lies.[7]

---

[5] Hopkins & Beard (2005) pp.34-35.
[6] Welch (2007) p.128 & Hopkins & Beard (2005) pp.36-39.
[7] Bomgardner (2000) pp.25-26.

This picture of the Colosseum shows part of the outer wall and the inner wall

M. Gilbert Hallier suggests that the design of the Colosseum was through the use of polycentric circular segments. In this design, the major and minor axes are laid out perpendicular, upon which the four centers of the circular segments would be laid out. By attaching appropriate lengths of rope to one of these centers, wall lines could be mapped out in both a radial and annular direction.

Another theory about how the Romans designed the Colosseum was put forth by Mark Wilson Jones. He suggests that Pythagorean triangles and inscribed circles were used, whereby the minor axis is divided into three equal parts. This involves the construction of a Pythagorean triangle, whose sides are in the ratios of 3:4:5. This produced a four-centered oval, and with the introduction of four additional circular segments, there were a total of eight circular segments, which produced the well-rounded shapes of the amphitheatre. Whatever plan was actually used, it is clear that there was meticulous surveying and planning involved, and that the Roman engineers and architects working on the Colosseum had a good grasp on the methods and techniques of construction.[8]

---

[8] Bomgardner (2000) pp.27-29.

Panorama shot of the Colosseum from the interior. Photo by Paolo Costa Baldi. License: GFDL/CC-BY-SA 3.

One reason the massive building continues to stand is because of its incredibly strong and solid foundations, but before the Colosseum could be constructed, Nero's artificial lake had to be drained. The lake was located in a river valley, so the unnamed architects of the Colosseum had to make sure there was proper drainage at all times. To accomplish this, they constructed a network of underground drains located around and through the amphitheatre. Although unseen, archaeological evidence shows that the drains were placed about 30 feet below the valley floor, and the water was carried off to the Tiber.

With proper drainage in place, the foundation could be poured. Rough estimates suggest that 30,000 tons of earth was removed in order to pour concrete and place cut stones to stabilize the amphitheatre and its upper stories. Arranged in the shape of a doughnut, the foundation depth beneath the walls and seating of the Colosseum runs about 40 feet and continues about 20 feet outside of the perimeter. Beneath the arena, the foundations are shallower, only running approximately 15 feet deep. After the foundation was finished, seven concentric "elliptical" rings were laid out, with each ring having 80 piers that rose into the air. Around these piers, the floors, vaults and tunnels began to form.[9]

---

[9] Bomgardner (2000) p.29, Welch (2007) p.134 & Hopkins & Beard (2005) p.142.

2013 photo of the interior by Bengt Nyman

Roman concrete was primarily used for the guts of the Colosseum, as it formed the foundation and the vaulting that was the basis for the arches, seating areas and the stairways. Meanwhile, brick was used for the facing of the arches and a few sections of the interior walls. Huge travertine blocks were used in the major load bearing parts of the amphitheatre and in areas where decorative carved stonework was required. Marble was also used to adorn the Colosseum and placed as facing, with larger blocks used for the seats and marble columns placed near the top of the structure. Lastly, iron was used in the construction of crampons, which bound the blocks of travertine together.[10]

A Roman spectator walking towards the Colosseum would first encounter a ring of bollards, which were small stone blocks (five of which still remain in situ) that were placed on the outer edge of the travertine pavement surrounding the amphitheatre. They were likely there to prevent vehicular traffic from getting near the Colosseum, and they may have been there as a way of slowing down and directing pedestrians who came to witness the day's events. Other people have theorized that they were anchors for the ropes tied to the awning atop the Colosseum, which provided interior shade for the spectators depending on the time of day. Although a plausible explanation Hopkins and Beard believe they were ill-suited for this task as the bollards had no deep foundations. Simply placed into the soil they were likely not strong enough to hold the heavy awning. Therefore it is more likely that they acted as some kind of traffic control guiding spectators to one of the entrances.[11]

---

[10] Bomgardner (2000) pp.29-30.
[11] Hopkins & Beard (2005) p.128 & Bomgardner (2000) p.5.

The Colosseum bollards

After passing the bollards, people entered a travertine paved piazza that surrounded the entire Colosseum and was approximately 65 feet wide. The pavement was not only decorative but functional as well, since it was a walking area free from mud. Bomgardner suspects that the piazza had peddlers selling wares, drinks and other souvenirs, similar to what the modern tourist might find visiting the Colosseum today. Of course, there were probably other people working there too; amongst the peddlers and spectators, pickpockets carefully made their way through the crowds, relieving many of their earnings. It was here that a Roman spectator could clearly see the façade of the towering monument.[12]

The exterior of the amphitheatre had four stories, three superimposed tiers of arcades and an attic, all of which soared about 170 feet total in height. Each tier had a different classical architectural order engaged within the façade, and the lowest tier had arched openings framed by engaged Tuscan columns resting on bases. The Tuscan column was the native Italian architectural order and was frequently used in old republican temples and some of the earliest stone amphitheatres found outside of Rome. The Colosseum was accessible by two steps that are now partially obscured by paving, which led to one of 80 archways. The northern entryway on the minor axis was uniquely marked apart from the other entrances, and the evidence shows traces of a shallow columnar porch and the remains of decorative stucco. Based on 1st century sculpture and coins depicting the Colosseum, above this porch there appears to have been a four-horse chariot (*quadriga*) carrying the emperor. Though nothing remains on the southern entryway on the minor axis of the Colosseum it is believed that it mimicked the northern one in

---

[12] Bomgardner (2000) p.6.

appearance and decorative arrangement. The other 78 archways leading into the Colosseum were all similar in appearance, and Roman numerals were inscribed above 76 of the archways in order to assist Roman spectators to their designated seats. The numerals started to the left of the northern entrance and moved counter-clockwise around the entire amphitheatre, skipping the entrances on both the minor and major axes. The fact that the other arches did not have Roman numerals suggests they may have been reserved entranceways.[13]

One of the arched entranceways. The Roman numeral LII (52) is still visible

Although there are no surviving texts or inscriptions naming the gates on the major axis, modern scholars often label the eastern gate "*Porta Libitinensis*", and the western gate "*Porta Triumphalis*" or "*Porta Sanivivaria*". The eastern gate is named after the goddess of death, Libitina, and it is suspected that dead gladiators were removed from the arena through this gate. The gate is mentioned in a late biography of the emperor Commodus, where it is told how his helmet is twice removed through the *Porta Libitinensis*, even though the author gives no indication as to which gate this was. The western gate, the *Porta Triumphalis*, was the other gate with access to the arena, and the name alludes to where the gladiators entered and the winners exited the arena. "*Porta Sanivivaria*" ("Gate of Life") is an alternative name for the western gate because the name was used in the eyewitness account of St. Perpetua's martyrdom, but in that case, the amphitheatre described was at Carthage in Tunisia, not the Colosseum in Rome. Therefore, it is impossible to say with certainty that these names were used for the two gates

---

[13] Welch (2007) p.136, Bomgardner (2000) p.9 & Hopkins & Beard (2005) pp.128-131.

leading into the Colosseum.[14]

When Vespasian died in 79 A.D., construction on the Colosseum had only reached the second level, and though Titus was now tasked with continuing its construction, the design plans do not seem to have changed. Separating the bottom tier from the second was a prominent protruding entablature that made it aesthetically pleasing to the eye. The façade of the second and third tier also mimicked that of the bottom, as each tier had 80 archways flanked by engaging columns. The difference with these tiers was that the engaged columns on the second level were of the Ionic order, while the engaged columns on the third level were of the Corinthian order. Another difference is that at the foot of each arch was a parapet wall, and behind these walls were high bases where statues would have stood. The statues had to be quite large in order for the Romans to be able to see them from the ground, so they may have stood at least 15 feet in height.

Although these statues no longer exist, coins and sculptural reliefs clearly indicate the presence of statues adorning the archways on the second and third levels of the Colosseum, and on one of these reliefs, dated to the Trajanic period (early 2nd century A.D.), there are a group of statues on the second and third levels that can be identified. On the second tier there is a statue of Hercules with his club and lion skin, a statue of Apollo leaning on the Delphic tripod, and a statue of a bearded Asclepius. The statues on the third level appear to be large birds posed in various positions, but other images from coins of the Colosseum suggest that the statues on the third level were of figures. This brings into question whether the statues depicted on the Trajanic funerary relief are completely accurate or are sculptural types preferred by the deceased. In either case, the evidence does seem to corroborate that statues adorned the archways of these two levels.[15]

The topmost level was the attic, which Domitian is believed to have finished. This section of the Colosseum was quite different in appearance compared to the first three tiers, but it is unclear if this was due to changes implemented by Domitian or if it had always been planned as such. The attic story appears as a wall with engaged Corinthian pilasters on pedestals, and these pilasters were aligned exactly over the columns from the lower levels. In between the pilasters were alternating square windows and shields. Although the shields are no longer on the attic, there are coins illustrating their presence there. The attic was also crowned by masts that secured the rigging for the awning (*velarium*) used to protect the spectators from the hot sun and drenching rain. These masts passed through holes in the crowning entablature and then set firmly into projecting corbels near the top of the attic story. There were three of these corbels between each set of Corinthian pilasters, and this system seems to have made the awning quite stable.[16]

---

[14] Hopkins & Beard (2005) pp.129-130.
[15] Bomgardner (2000) p.6 & Welch (2007) pp.135-137.
[16] Bomgardner (2000) p.6 & Welch (2007) p.136.

Jean-Léon Gérôme's *Ave Caesar Morituri te Salutant* imagines the Colosseum, with the awning appearing at the top.

Not only was the Colosseum the largest of its kind, but the façade was a mixture of styles never before seen in amphitheatre construction. Usually built by soldiers in their legionary camps, the earliest amphitheatres typically had a plain façade, while those with decorative elements possessed at most only the Tuscan column, the native Italian order. However, the Colosseum incorporated Greek decorative column orders and the Greeks and Etruscan technique of framing arches with engaged half-columns. The Romans took these decorative techniques to their highest degree, thus making it their own. Incorporating these decorative elements on the Colosseum symbolized that previous facilities that provided plain entertainment were no longer acceptable; the entertainment facility was being elevated thereafter as an important Roman structure.[17]

---

[17] Bomgardner (2000) pp.6-9 & Welch (2007) pp.138-141.

The Interior of the Colosseum

Photo of the interior by Jean-Pol Grandmont

Once a Roman spectator entered the Colosseum, they could use one of the four circular galleries (*ambulacra*) on the lowest floor to easily move laterally around the amphitheatre. Two of these galleries were located near the exterior of the structure, with another situated in the middle and the last one close to the arena. The second and third level of the Colosseum each had two exterior galleries as well. All of the galleries were barrel vaulted, except for the inner gallery on the second level, which was groin vaulted, and though the lowest floor had a middle and an inner gallery, the second floor is the only other level with an inner gallery. All of the galleries allowed spectators to easily move around the amphitheatre and were suitable locations for stretching during intermissions. Furthermore, the galleries also provided support for the seats above.[18]

Each of the 80 entrances into the Colosseum provided access to a radial passageway, which either led directly to stairways leading up to the second level, to lower tiered seating, or to one of the interior circular passageways. A few of the radial passageways also led to cul-de-sacs, but this was rare in the Colosseum. Sprinkled throughout the Colosseum were numerous water fountains for the spectators, and scholars speculate there must have been lavatories within the structure, but no archaeological evidence for any has ever been found.[19]

The Colosseum was specifically planned so each person could easily and quickly access their designated seat. This was accomplished by going through one of the 76 numbered entryways. Depending on the level where a Roman spectator sat, one simply had to go through the proper

---

[18] Welch (2007) pp.134-135 & Bomgardner (2000) p.9.
[19] Bomgardner (2000) p.9 & Hopkins & Beard (2005) p.128.

entryway and use the connected passages and stairways to easily get to their seat. As previously mentioned, the entranceways on the minor and major axes of the Colosseum did not have numerals placed above them, likely because these entrances were reserved for special individuals. The entrances on the minor axis led to special reserved boxes, the best seats in the amphitheatre, while the entrances on the major axis led directly into the arena. The southern box on the minor axis could also be accessed by a subterranean tunnel.[20]

Remains of the seating in the Colosseum. Photo by Russell Yarwood

---

[20] Bomgardner (2000) p.9.

Diagram of the seating plan for the Colosseum.

Romans sitting at the podium, the seating area immediately adjacent to the arena, could take one of the 44 entrances leading directly to the innermost circular gallery, and from there they could take one of the 12 staircases leading up to an arched entrance (*vomitorium*) and through onto the podium, where there were seven rows of marble seats. The next section for spectators, directly above the podium and its seven rows, was 12 rows of marble of seats. Romans had two options to get to these seats, depending whether or not they sat in the lower or upper rows. The lower rows of seats could be reached through 16 stairways from the middle circular passageway, located between the inner and the two exterior circular passageways on the ground floor. Access to the upper rows was more indirect. From the same middle passageway Romans climbed one of the thirty-six stairways to the two exterior galleries of the second floor. From here they walked to the inner passageway on this floor and ascended one of the twenty short staircases through the *vomitorium* and to their seats.[21]

Spectators sitting in the next section of marble seats, totaling 19 rows, could access the lower rows of seats by climbing one of the stairways from the innermost exterior passageway of the second floor. Romans then exited through the *vomitorium* to find their seats. Those sitting in the higher rows had to ascend one of the 16 stairways leading from the inner passageway of the second floor to a small covered gallery located between the second and third floors of the

---

[21] Bomgardner (2000) pp.9-12.

amphitheatre. This was directly above the innermost gallery of the exterior galleries of the second floor, and from that point, spectators climbed one of 16 stairways to the arcaded gallery of the third floor and then out through the *vomitorium* to access the upper rows.[22]

Access to the lower rows of seats in the next section, consisting of seven limestone rows, was through a T-shaped stairway from the innermost passageway of the third floor. A T-shaped stairway consisted of two lateral ascending stairways that joined a single stairway ascending inwards. In order to reach the top rows of this section, Romans ascended one of 16 T-shaped stairways from the outermost passageway of the third floor and out through a *vomitorium* to their seats.

Photo of an arched entryway by Bengt Nyman

Those making their way to the last and topmost section of the amphitheatre used one of the same 16 T-shaped stairways leaving the outermost passageway of the third floor. However,

---
[22] Bomgardner (2000) p.13.

rather than ascending the inward stairway heading towards the limestone seats, spectators got off at the top of the lateral portion of the T-shaped stairway onto the attic gallery of the fourth floor. From here Romans ascended another T-shaped stairway that led to the last gallery of the amphitheatre. In front of the six wooden rows of seats here were colonnades supporting a roof that covered the spectators sitting all the way up there.[23]

Stationed on the roof of this last gallery were sailors who managed the retractable *velarium* awning, which not only protected the spectators from sun and rain but may have also allowed air to circulate and create a cool breeze. It is believed that this awning extended out over the seats of the Colosseum with perhaps only the area directly above the arena left open. The wooden masts tied to the awning were attached to the attic story and supported by the crowning entablature, giving it good stability against the wind.[24]

Once Romans had their tickets, they could proceed to their seats, but how these tickets were distributed to people is not entirely clear. It is probable that the majority of tickets were given to the emperor's clients, upon which the tickets would then filter downwards to the lower Roman social classes. This distribution was probably linked to the patron system of Roman society, I which members of a lower class would attach themselves as clients to a more powerful upper class patron. A patron would protect his clients in a number of ways, including helping with business or giving gifts, while clients would help their patron by supporting them during elections or in business. Therefore, a patron could give his clients tickets for the amphitheatre shows, which were then given to their clients and so forth.[25]

Once spectators had their tickets, they could easily find their seats by simply proceeding through the numbered entryway that corresponded to the number on their ticket. Exactly where a spectator sat within the Colosseum depended upon the person's social status. Although there are no literary sources specifically outlining the seating arrangements within Roman amphitheatres, there is mention of where people sat within Roman theatres. This, coupled with inscriptional evidence, including some from the stone seats of amphitheatres, shows that the seating arrangement of the amphitheatre was the same or very similar to that of the theatre.[26]

Better seats were for the upper class, which meant being closer to the arena, and the two best seats in the house were located on the minor axis of the Colosseum. The northern entrance adorned with the *quadriga* is believed to have given direct access to a box reserved for the empress and her female attendants, which may have included the Vestal virgins and other important magistrates. Meanwhile, the southern entrance is thought to have led to the box reserved for the emperor, his retinue, special guests and other male members of the family. The belief that this box might have been reserved for the emperor is due in part to a subterranean gallery connecting this box to the outside of the amphitheatre, which would have allowed the emperor to quickly enter and exit the Colosseum or to safely bypass Romans who might wish him harm. The seats in these two boxes were visible to everyone within the amphitheatre, so it's not surprising that the emperor, his wife and their attendants sat at these locations. The two entrances on the major axis also allowed direct access to the arena and were likely used by performers and other arena attendants, such as those bringing animals or props that were going to be used for the day's events.[27]

---

[23] Bomgardner (2000) p.13.
[24] Quennell (1971) p.36 & Bomgardner (2000) p.6.
[25] Ward, Heichelheim & Yeo (2014) p.45 & Bomgardner (2000) p.6.
[26] Suetonius, *Divus Augustus*.44, Martial, *Epigrams*.5.8 & Bomgardner (2000) p.17.
[27] Hopkins & Beard (2005) pp.133-144 & Bomgardner (2000) p.9.

The next best seats in the Colosseum were the seven marble rows located just behind the podium, where the senators, priests of the more important religious cults and distinguished foreign guests or ambassadors sat. Senators were likely seated in specific rows based upon certain criteria, which may have included whether they came from a patrician or plebeian family or whether they held an important office, such as a consulship. It's almost certain that the most important senators sat closest to the emperor near the minor axis of the Colosseum.

The podium, as it survives today, is believed to belong to a later construction phase of the Colosseum. As the number of senators, which was around 600 in the early 1st century A.D., continued to increase, by the 4th century the seven rows of seats would no longer have accommodated the 2,000 members of the senate. With the construction of the podium and the seven original rows behind it, scholars have calculated that this area could accommodate around 2,070 spectators.[28]

The section above the senators was allotted to the Order of the Knights, and with 12 rows, approximately 11,700 spectators filled this level of the Colosseum. Similar to the seating arrangements of the senators, knights were likely also placed according to status, based on salary, honorific distinctions, appointments or overall wealth. This may have even included placing all those knights who went bankrupt in the same section, as stipulated in a piece of legislation from 67 B.C. (*lex Roscia*) regarding seats in the theatre. By carefully arranging the knights and senators accordingly, every Roman in the amphitheatre would clearly know whose careers or fortunes were doing well and whose were not. Thus, if someone's seat improved, spectators would know that person's power and status was rising, and the opposite would be apparent as well.[29]

The next section of 19 rows allowed for approximately 20,400 spectators, and Roman male citizens with sufficient wealth sat in this section of the Colosseum. The seats were further divided according to marital status, soldiers, or minors accompanied by their tutors, as was the case in the theatre. Rank may have also factored into arranging the seats, but there is no surviving information that provides these details.

In the next section, the urban poor, slaves, foreign residents, and freed slaves sat on the seven available rows. Calculations estimate that approximately 10,100 spectators occupied these seats high up in the amphitheatre. Unlike the lower levels, the seats in this section may not have been reserved according to status or rank, so when spectators arrived they probably chose the best unfilled seats.[30]

The very last and highest seats in the amphitheatre were six rows reserved for the important ladies of Rome, which included the wives and daughters of senators, knights and important Roman citizens. There are potentially many reasons the women sat all the way up there. The colonnaded gallery offered the most protection from the weather, and perhaps equally as important was the fact that these ladies were sheltered from the prying eyes of men, thanks to the wall separating this section from the one below. Another potential reason for placing such esteemed ladies here was the belief that women were much more sensitive to bloodshed and therefore should be protected from such gruesome sights.

Some historians have speculated that one reason women were seated so high in the Colosseum was to minimize any potential interaction between them and the gladiators, who were known as heart-throbs and personified virility in the Roman world. Respected men may have feared their

---

[28] Bomgardner (2000) pp.12, 17-18.
[29] Bomgardner (2000) p.13.
[30] Bomgardner (2000) p.13.

wives falling in love with a gladiator, so to avoid such an embarrassing situation, placing them as far from the gladiators as possible would've been a good idea. The Roman writer Juvenal wrote about this phenomenon: "What was the youthful charm that so fired Eppia? What hooked her? What did she see in him to make her put up with being called 'the gladiator's moll'? Her poppet, her Sergius, was no chicken, with a dud arm that prompted hope of early retirement. Besides his face looked a proper mess, helmet-scarred, a great wart on his nose, an unpleasant discharge always trickling from one eye. But he was a gladiator. That word makes the whole breed seem handsome, and made her prefer him to her children and country, her sister, her husband. Steel is what they fall in love with."

Furthermore, by seating them so high, which required a climb of approximately 220 stairs, many women might not have thought it worthwhile to attend the spectacles, thereby freeing the men from their spouses for at least several hours.[31] Either way, these rows of seats could accommodate approximately 10,300 spectators, meaning that the Colosseum in total could hold around 55,000 spectators.[32]

The organization of spectators according to social status was not only done vertically in the amphitheatre but horizontally as well. The interior was arranged so that only upper class spectators would need to go deep within the Colosseum, such as senators who needed access to the innermost circular passageway to get to their seats. The knights, ranked just below the senators, needed to access their seats from the middle gallery, whereas the remainder of Romans had no need to go beyond the exterior circular passageways because their seats could be reached from the stairways located here. Therefore, just as the seats closest to the arena were reserved for the wealthy, the innermost space of the Colosseum was as well. For the lower orders of Roman society, the exterior passageways and stairs were strictly for their usage, as the highest seats were for them. Essentially, the Colosseum was important not just for staging spectacles but for also reinforcing the social hierarchy of Roman society. It was a place where the elite men of Rome could display their power for all to see, with better seats literally symbolizing superior status.[33]

A visitor to the Colosseum today will immediately notice that the arena floor no longer remains, and all that can be seen are subterranean galleries (*hypogeum*). When these galleries were constructed is not entirely clear, but it is thought they were constructed during the reign of the emperor Domitian between 81-96 A.D. and thus not a part of the original construction. Below the arena floor is a two level subterranean gallery containing corridors, storerooms, hoists and cages. The lowest level had 32 cages that housed animals until they were needed in the amphitheatre, and when required, the cages could be hoisted to the next level through one of 80 shafts. Once prompted, the animals would be freed and driven up ramps towards trap doors leading to the arena floor. In addition to animals, stage props, mechanical devices, gladiators, hunters and condemned individuals could also be introduced into the arena at any designated moment. Given the noise of the crowds, the thuds of combatants on the arena floor, the roaring or whimpering of the animals in their cages and the sounds of those working, the subterranean gallery was likely very loud. Throw in the darkness, smoke from oil lamps, and heat from sweating workers, and this was definitely not a pleasant place to work or be in.[34]

---

[31] Köhne & Ewigleben (2000) p.132, Welch (2007) p.159 & Bomgardner (2000) pp.13-14.
[32] Bomgardner (2000) p.13.
[33] Welch (2007) p.159 & Bomgardner (2000) p.14.
[34] Hopkins & Beard (2005) pp.136-137 & Bomgardner (2000) pp.21-22.

2013 photo of the *hypogeum* by Bengt Nyman

The subterranean galleries are actually wider than the arena floor, because there are extending storerooms at each end of the major axis. Furthermore the storerooms on the east end have an underground corridor leading to a gladiatorial school located just outside of the Colosseum called the *Ludus Magnus*. There were other underground corridors on the minor axis as well, with one leading north and one leading south. These were possibly used to bring animals directly to their cages under the arena.[35]

Although nothing remains of the actual arena floor, it is possible to reconstruct what it may have looked like in antiquity based on archaeological remains. The arena floor likely consisted mostly of wooden planks covered over with sand, which was used because it soaked up spilled blood and other fluids and gave the combatants a solid footing while fighting. Another benefit was that soiled sand could easily be removed to ensure the cleanliness of the arena and to minimize the spread of disease.[36]

The wall surrounding the arena floor was almost 12 feet high, which was a fairly safe distance from the action down below, but one issue with such a high wall was that if gladiators fought near it, some spectators would be unable to see them. This problem could also occur when animals were released into the arena. Sometimes, bewildered and scared animals sought the darkness and protection of the arena, which prevented some in the crowd from being able to see them. In order to eliminate these blind spots for spectators sitting high in the Colosseum, large posts were inserted into the arena floor a certain distance from the arena wall, and in between them a net was strung that acted as a barrier. The net did not block anyone's view, and as an additional safety feature, it prevented animals from jumping into the crowds. Between this net

---

[35] Bomgardner (2000) pp.21-22 & Hopkins & Beard (2005) pp.136-137.
[36] Bomgardner (2000) p.21.

and the arena wall was a marble walkway, so when animals sought the safety of the net, Colosseum attendants could poke and prod them back into the center of the arena.[37]

This was not the only safety measure implemented to keep animals from trying to escape the arena or attacking a senator sitting in the front row. The slabs of polished marble that covered the arena wall were not only luxurious decorations but also made the wall a very slippery surface to climb. Also, overhanging the top of the arena wall were horizontal ivory rollers that spun on their shafts, making it nearly impossible for any animal to get a proper foothold. Lastly, positioned around the arena wall were archers who were watching and ready to shoot down any animals that managed to get past the other defenses. All of these measures meant every Roman could see the action happening in the arena and that the upper class was well protected from the dangerous activities occurring below them.[38]

Obtaining and Training Gladiators

Although gladiators could become very popular among their contemporaries, and today they are among the most romanticized characters in Roman history, they typically belonged to the lowest Roman social order either due to being prisoners of war, slaves or criminals. Those who were prisoners of war came from the many different parts of the world that had been conquered by the Romans, and in fact some of the earliest Republican gladiators were actually modeled and named after the warriors of some of these conquered cultures, such as the Gauls, Samnites and Thracians. The most famous gladiator of all, Spartacus, was a Thracian, and Plutarch wrote quite admiringly in his *Life of Crassus*, "Spartacus was chief, a Thracian of one of the nomad tribes, and a man not only of high spirit and valiant, but in understanding, also, and in gentleness, superior to his condition, and more of a Grecian than the people of his country usually are." This was quite high praise considering the fact that Plutarch himself was Greek.

Livy also noted how gladiators were occasionally dressed up to resemble conquered peoples in his seminal history of Rome: "The war in Samnium, immediately afterwards, was attended with equal danger and an equally glorious conclusion. The enemy, besides their other warlike preparation, had made their battle-line to glitter with new and splendid arms. There were two corps: the shields of the one were inlaid with gold, of the other with silver...The Romans had already heard of these splendid accoutrements, but their generals had taught them that a soldier should be rough to look on, not adorned with gold and silver but putting his trust in iron and in courage...The Dictator, as decreed by the senate, celebrated a triumph, in which by far the finest show was afforded by the captured armor. So the Romans made use of the splendid armor of their enemies to do honour to their gods; while the Campanians, in consequence of their pride and in hatred of the Samnites, equipped after this fashion the gladiators who furnished them entertainment at their feasts, and bestowed on them the name Samnites."

Many condemned criminals were given a sentence to become gladiators, but not every condemned criminal was given this sentence. In fact, most met justice by being tossed to wild animals, executed by crucifixion or burned alive in the arena. Those who were sentenced to become gladiators at least had the possibility of surviving, especially if they turned out to have a knack for fighting.

The last resource for recruiting gladiators came in the form of slaves. Runaway slaves or those who displeased their masters could be sold to a gladiatorial school, but in order to prevent owners from making some quick cash by selling their slaves during the 2nd century A.D., the Roman emperor Hadrian forbade the sale of a slave to a gladiatorial school unless the slave had

---

[37] Köhne & Ewigleben (2000) p.35 & Bomgardner (2000) p.21.
[38] Hopkins & Beard (2005) p.135 & Bomgardner (2000) p.21.

committed an offense that justified this action. The status and influence of slaves could be as varied as that of free men in the Roman Republic. Slaves could be scholars, doctors, tutors to the children of the wealthy, and even persons of vast influence in their own right, such as the personal companions of senators and patricians. Slaves could eventually earn their freedom, or be granted such status in their owner's will. At the same time, however, it is important not to forget that slaves were quite literally property, possessing no rights before the law. Slaves could legally be killed, tortured, starved or sexually assaulted, in the same way a person today would be entitled to destroy their own legally purchased car. Moreover, it is worth noting that while house slaves might live pleasant or even pampered lives, depending on their qualifications or the wealth of their owner, unskilled laborers were subjected to an existence of minimal food and comfort, and they often died young and badly. If a slave attempted to escape, crucifixion was a common method of punishment as a gruesomely theatrical way of warning other slaves. The crucified victim would linger in agony for days until they either died of thirst or suffered progressively more severe cramps that would lock down their lungs and make them die of slow suffocation. To some, this dire fate might still have seemed preferable to a continued existence of constant hunger, exposure, hardship and backbreaking labor, but clearly having a chance to survive as a gladiator was even better.

Although the majority of gladiators were plucked from these social classes, free Roman citizens could volunteer to become gladiators as well. The reasons for a free citizen to join varied, but it included participating for the thrill of danger, needing a source of income, or even seeking and obtaining fame and glory. There is also plenty of evidence that some women fought as gladiators; the Roman writer Juvenal wrote about one woman named Mevia hunting in the arena "with spear in hand and breasts exposed". Juvenal also expanded on the theme at length in his satire:

"Who has not seen the dummies of wood they slash at and batter
Whether with swords or with spears, going through all the manoeuvres?
These are the girls who blast on the trumpets in honour of Flora.
Or, it may be they have deeper designs, and are really preparing
For the arena itself. How can a woman be decent
Sticking her head in a helmet, denying the sex she was born with?
Manly feats they adore, but they wouldn't want to be men,
Poor weak things (they think), how little they really enjoy it!
What a great honour it is for a husband to see, at an auction
Where his wife's effects are up for sale, belts, shin-guards,
Arm-protectors and plumes!
Hear her grunt and groan as she works at it, parrying, thrusting;
See her neck bent down under the weight of her helmet.
Look at the rolls of bandage and tape, so her legs look like tree-trunks,
Then have a laugh for yourself, after the practice is over,
Armor and weapons put down, and she squats as she used the vessel.
Ah, degenerate girls from the line of our praetors and consuls,
Tell us, whom have you seen got up in any such fashion,
Panting and sweating like this? No gladiator's wench,
No tough strip-tease broad would ever so much as attempt it."

A relief depicting two female gladiators found at Halicarnassus. The art named the women Amazonia and Achillia.

Some of the Roman emperors were so thrilled by the games that they also wanted to be gladiators, which no doubt fascinated and pleased the Roman public but offered a bit of a headache logistically. Naturally, the inherent dangers of gladiatorial combat had to be contained if the emperor was participating. Caligula loved the games, and Commodus was such a fan that he would actually participate in combat at the ludus, the gladiator school. Commodus began referring to himself as "Hercules Reborn", and he hunted animals in the arena. On one statue, Commodus had it inscribed, "Champion of secutores; only left-handed fighter to conquer twelve times one thousand men."

That said, the practice of free Roman citizens becoming gladiators was looked down upon, and the Romans continually discouraged their citizens from doing so. Many emperors went so far as to enact laws preventing Romans from joining gladiatorial schools, and in 11 A.D. an age restriction was placed on freeborn men (25 years of age) and women (20 years of age) before they could join a gladiator school. This apparently did not work, so another decree was issued in 19 A.D. forbidding women of the upper class to become gladiators. The fact that these decrees were enacted at all demonstrates the growing interest Romans had in volunteering to become gladiators.

Once a person joined a gladiatorial school, he had to swear an oath "to endure being burned by fire, bound in chains, beaten, and killed by the sword", and by swearing this oath the gladiator gained some form of honor because he was sacrificing everything for the arena. The gladiatorial schools could be run privately or by the state, and the man in charge of the school was called the *lanista*. The *lanista* was responsible for acquiring gladiators, organizing their training and then selling or renting them out for shows. The city of Rome had four gladiator schools by the end of the 1st century A.D., the most significant of which was the Great School (*Ludus Magnus*), located right next to the Colosseum. The school even had an underground tunnel connecting to the great amphitheatre in order to shuttle gladiators to the arena quickly.

There were many other schools throughout the Roman Empire, and some of them could focus on training specific types of gladiators. For example the Gallic School (*Ludus Gallicus*) trained the *murmillo* gladiator type, one of a number of gladiator types categorized by appearance, weapons and fighting style. Depending on the size of the school, it typically consisted of an arena or field for practicing combat, cells for the gladiators, apartment rooms for the staff, medical facilities, a kitchen, dining room and a place to store the various pieces of gladiatorial equipment, which included both the wooden practice swords and the real metal ones. The staff of the gladiatorial schools included combat trainers (who were usually active or ex-gladiators), psychological trainers, doctors, cooks and masseurs. Once adequately trained, the gladiators would be ready for real combat.[39]

One of the best descriptions of a *lanista* came from Plutarch's writings about what prompted Spartacus to lead a rebellion that started in a *ludus*. He explained, "One Lentulus Batiates trained up a great many gladiators in Capua, most of them Gauls and Thracians, who, not for any fault by them committed, but simply through the cruelty of their master, were kept in confinement for this object of fighting one with another. Two hundred of these formed a plan to escape, but their plot being discovered, those of them who became aware of it in time to anticipate their master, being seventy-eight, got out of a cook's shop chopping-knives and spits, and made their way through the city, and lighting by the way on several wagons that were carrying gladiator's arms to another city, they seized upon them and armed themselves."

---

[39] Shadrake (2005) pp.69-83, Nossov (2009) pp.142-145, Dunkle (2008) pp.30-30-58, Wiedemann (1992) pp.102-124.

The Different Kinds of Gladiators

A mosaic depicting gladiators fighting.

Many different gladiator types existed in the Roman world, but even though gladiator combats began during the Roman Republican period, the information regarding these early gladiator types is not as well-known as that from the Imperial period, when gladiatorial combat became more popular and better organized. Below are the descriptions of the different known gladiator types that existed at some point during the Imperial Age, excluding the *bestiarius* and *venator* classes, special gladiators who were used only for the animal shows and never fought other men.

The *Andabata*

The *andabata* gladiator existed only in the Roman Republican period, and there is no information suggesting that this class continued into the Imperial period. In fact, very little is actually known about this type except for the peculiar fact that they fought blind; the helmet of the *andabata* was close fitting and had no openings for the eyes. It is unclear what kind of armor they wore, but presumably it was metal, or otherwise the fight could end quickly given their lack of vision. The *andabata* fought gladiators from the same class and victory was presumably based on chance, as the fighter had to rely on his ears and possibly the helpful shouting from spectators.

Given the unusual nature of this type of gladiator, it is probable that the *andabata* was not actually a class of gladiator but rather a term used to describe any gladiator with his specialized armor and weapons who wore a helmet that prevented him from seeing. For example, some sources mention an *eques* gladiator blinded by his helmet riding into the arena sitting backwards on his horse, leading many to assume that fights involving them were probably rare and performed more for comedic entertainment than a serious bout between combatants.[40]

The *Arbelas/Scissor*

The *arbelas* is believed to have once been the *Scissor*, a gladiator type that existed during the Roman Republican period. The *scissor* class of gladiator was either discontinued or had its name changed by the time the Roman Imperial period began, and many believe the latter case is most likely. Regardless of this, this class is still sometimes referred to as the *scissor*.

Not much is known about the *arbelas* type of gladiator because there are only six known images of it, and the majority of these come from the eastern part of the empire. The name of this gladiator comes from the semi-circular knife that a shoemaker would use and was likely one of his primary weapons. The images depicting this gladiator show that the *arbelas* fought other gladiators of the same type and occasionally the *retiarius* gladiator.[41]

Illustration of the weapon.

These types of gladiators were protected by a close fitting helmet with a visor, an armguard on the right arm and short greaves going up to the knee on both legs. The images also show that the body could be covered by scale armor or ringmail that went down almost to the knees. Some of the helmets appear to have a crest on the top, but the shape of the helmet is difficult to determine with accuracy.

The *arbelas* did not carry a shield but instead held a rather unusual weapon in his left hand. This weapon appears to have been an armored forearm piece with a crescent-shaped blade on the end, and it may have been sharpened along both the outer and inner surfaces, thereby allowing it to easily cut the nets of the *retiarius*. However, this weapon may have been awkward and flimsy too, because in two of the images it lies on the ground, suggesting it had been discarded by its gladiator. It is still unclear exactly how this weapon was fashioned since there are no surviving examples from the archaeological record. The other hand was equipped with a dagger with what appears in the images as a straight blade.[42]

The *Crupellarius*

---

[40] Nossov (2009) pp.70-71 & Shadrake (2005) p.154.
[41] Shadrake (2005) p.172 & Nossov (2009) pp.45-47.
[42] Nossov (2009) pp.47-48.

These gladiators are believed to have originated in Gaul and were limited to that province, but they were also mentioned by the ancient Roman historian Tacitus, who described them fighting against Roman legions in 21 A.D.:

> "There was also a party of slaves training to be gladiators. Completely encased in iron in the national fashion, the *crupellarii*, as they were called, were too clumsy for offensive purposes but impregnable in defence... the infantry made a frontal attack. The Gallic flanks were driven. The iron-clad contingent caused some delay as their casing resisted javelins and swords. However the Romans used axes and mattocks and struck at their plating and its wearers like men demolishing a wall. Others knocked down the immobile gladiators with poles or pitchforks, and, lacking the power to rise, they were left for dead."[43]

Based on this description, it seems the *crupellarius* was heavily armored, including being possibly protected by articulated iron strips covering most of the body. For the most part, this made them useless in battle. One image discovered in France might depict this type of gladiator. Although the gladiator appears to be entirely clad in armor, only the helmet is clearly seen. It appears as a medieval pot, but with several holes presumably for ventilation and light. There also appears to be a projection in the shape of a nose. The weapons of the *crupellarius* are unknown, as is his typical opponent in the Gallic arena.[44]

The *Dimachaerus*

There are very few literary sources mentioning the *dimachaerus* gladiator, and images of it are contradictory and therefore frequently disputed. *Dimachaerus* means "armed with two blades", referring possibly to swords or daggers, and thus it was certainly a gladiator who was equipped with two weapons. The *dimachaerus* presumably fought others from the same gladiator class.

Historian Konstantin Nossov believes that there is only one relief that portrays a *dimachaerus* from the early 3rd century A.D., and based on that image, this gladiator type wore a broad-brimmed helmet with greaves covering just below the knee on both legs. He is wearing either a tunic or metal armor, but the latter seems most likely since there was no other form of protection. The relief shows that the *dimachaerus* carried short sword-daggers in each hand, with one having a curved blade.

Besides this relief, there are other images of the *dimachaerus* gladiator, although they provide contradictory evidence. For example, one image shows a *retiarius* holding two daggers and a trident, while another shows a gladiator armed with two daggers and a shield. This has led some to believe that the *dimachaerus* was not a specific gladiator class but simply a term used to describe any gladiator armed with two weapons. However, Nossov argues that the *dimachaerus* has epigraphic evidence to support its existence and is mentioned as a class type by the 2nd century A.D. Greek writer Artemidorus in his work called the *Oneirocritica*. Therefore, it is logical to presume that the *dimachaerus* was indeed a gladiator class in the Roman Imperial period.[45]

The *Eques*

The name of this gladiator derives from the Latin word for horse. The *eques*, or "rider", entered the arena on horseback and was armed with a lance or spear, as shown on some surviving images dating to the Imperial period. This gladiator fought on horseback only briefly though, as most

---

[43] Tacitus, *Annales*,3.43. Translation from Shadrake (2005) p.184.
[44] Shadrake (2005) pp.183-184, Nossov (2009) p.71, Dunkle (2008) p.118 & Junkelmann (2000) p.63.
[45] Nossov (2009) p.57, Junkelmann (2000) p.63 & Artemidorus, *Oneirocritica*, 2.32.

images show the *eques* engaging in combat dismounted. This suggests that these gladiators quickly got off their horses in order to fight hand to hand combat, similar to the other gladiator types. The *eques* only fought gladiators from the same class, and they may have opened the gladiatorial events by starting at either end of the arena to attack each other.

The *eques* gladiator in the Republican period wore protective scale armor, but images from the Imperial period suggest this changed to simply sleeveless tunics that ended just above the knees. These tunics had two narrow vertical stripes of different colors that ran down the garment, harkening back to the dress of the Republican equestrian class. They wore a broad-brimmed helmet with a visor and occasionally there was a feather on either side, but they never had a central plume. The shield was medium sized and approximately 60 centimeters in diameter, which was typical for a cavalryman of the Republican period. The *eques* had an armguard on his right arm, and his legs were sometimes protected by gaiters or leg wrappings. The first weapon an *eques* used was a spear measuring 6-7 feet long, but he was also equipped with a sword to be used after he dismounted. Spectators could differentiate between the gladiators because each wore a different colored tunic or carried a different colored shield.[46]

Drawing depicting an eques

The *Essedarius*

The name of this gladiator translates as "charioteer", and as the Latin word *essedum* suggests, they fought from a light two-wheeled Celtic chariot. In other words, this gladiator type was inspired by foreign soldiers who Julius Caesar described in a passage: "[The chariot fighters] ride about everywhere throwing spears and create much panic in [our] ranks because of their horses and the sound made by the wheels, and when they have made their way among the troops of [Roman] cavalry, they jump down from their chariots and fight on foot."[47]

The *essedarius* gladiator was well known by the mid-1st century B.C. and continued into the Roman Imperial period, but even though the *essedarius* is frequently mentioned in literary

---
[46] Nossov (2009) p.70, Junkelmann (2000) pp.47-48, Dunkle (2008) pp.99-100 & Shadrake (2005) pp.151-154.
[47] Julius Caesar, *Bell.Gall.*4.33.1. Translation taken from Dunkle (2008) p.114.

sources and on inscriptions, there are no images that can be positively identified as this type of gladiator. Junkelmann argues that as the *essedarius* was increasingly mentioned on inscriptions, visual representations of this gladiator must have increased as well, thus speculating that any gladiator in Roman art whose equipment does not conform to the other well-known types must be an *essedarius* gladiator. Based on Junkelmann's assumption, this gladiator wore a close fitting helmet with feathers, an armguard on his right arm, padding on his legs, and was armed with a sword and an oval shield. None of these supposedly *essedarii* gladiators are ever shown on a chariot, which has led many scholars to argue that like the *eques* gladiator, after entering the arena in their chariots the combatants quickly dismounted and fought on foot. An alternative theory is that perhaps the chariot was abandoned altogether but the name of these gladiators remained.

It is believed that the primary opponent of the *essedarius* was against another *essedarius*. However, if the images of the *essedarii* have been correctly identified, then they may have fought against the *retiarius* gladiator as well. Nossov reasons that the *retiarius* would have had an advantage over the *essedarius* because the latter was very susceptible to the trident, so he believes that perhaps the few images portraying these pairings were simply early experiments before the *secutor* became the primary opponent of the *retiarius*.[48]

The *Gallus*

The *gallus* gladiator is named after the Gauls, the enemy tribes from France, but despite the fact the Gauls were well-known among the Romans and the *gallus* is mentioned in literary sources, there are no surviving identifiable images of this class, making it difficult to determine how they were equipped in the arena. It is presumed that this gladiator was the forerunner to the *murmillo* class, and because of this, Nossov believes that a *gallus* gladiator was equipped with a large shield, a helmet, at least one greave and a sword. However, others, such as historian Susanna Shadrake, believe a *gallus* would have closely followed the appearance of a real Gallic warrior. A Gallic warrior typically wore no helmet, and though some wore armor, others were bare-chested. They also carried a large oval or rectangular shield and were armed with a sword or spear. This appearance is based on their portrayals as captives of war in Roman art, but however the *gallus* gladiator was equipped, it first appeared in the mid-1st century B.C. and was gone by the mid-1st century A.D.[49]

The *Gladiatrix* (female gladiator)

The spectacle of females fighting in the arena was limited to the Imperial period. By the end of the Republican period, women, particularly upper class women, were beginning to gain more freedom to pursue their own desires, and for some of these women, one of their desires was performing as a gladiator, despite being considered a degrading occupation for aristocrats. Swept up by the romance of the arena, impressionable aristocratic young women (and men) continually volunteered to fight in the arena. Even after decrees were made in 11 and 19 A.D. to discourage Romans from becoming gladiators, literary sources indicate that in the 1st and 2nd centuries A.D., females continued to volunteer as gladiators. The upper class women who freely volunteered were thought to have brought shame to their families, but if the women were from the lower classes it was not considered as scandalous. Not all females participated willingly, as some emperors, such as Nero, would force upper class women to fight as gladiators or beast hunters.[50]

---

[48] Dunkle (2008) pp.113-114, Nossov (2009) pp.75-77 & Junkelmann (2000) p.63.
[49] Nossov (2009) pp.71-72 & Shadrake (2005) pp.142-143.
[50] Dunkle (2008) pp.118-123, Shadrake (2005) pp.185-195 & Nossov (2009) pp.148-149.

Without question, some of the recorded events involving female gladiators were for the amusement of the crowds. For example Domitian, had female gladiators fighting dwarves in the arena during one of his sponsored games. Since dwarves were typically shown to provoke laughter, this event was likely not considered a serious gladiator combat, but there were definitely serious gladiator bouts as well, as indicated by the relief depicting Amazonia and Achillia fighting one another. The accompanying inscription specifies that they were both released after their fight, indicating that the sponsor of the show thought the two fought well enough to have the battle declared a draw, and thus both were allowed to leave the arena alive. This example shows that women did participate in serious lethal combat.

The image of the two *gladiatrices* is not clear enough to determine the type of gladiator class they belonged to, if any. Both females are depicted as heavily armed, equipped with a rectangular shield, armguard, greaves and short sword. They appear to be bare-breasted, which may have been to clearly show their gender or because male gladiators also fought typically without chest armor. Each has a helmet, but it lies on the ground, and there is not enough detail to determine the exact type.

Based on the surviving details, suggestions of their gladiator class include the *provocator* and *thraex*. The medium rectangular shield is reminiscent of the *thraex* gladiators, but that class did not typically fight one another and their primary armament was a curved weapon, not a short sword. A problem with identifying them as *provacatores* is that they have no chest armor, which is characteristic of this gladiator class. Of course, females may not have belonged to any of the male gladiator types and instead were categorized according to different weapon and armor specifications. Therefore, the *gladiatrix* may not have ever been included among the official gladiator classes; female gladiators may have been more of an entertaining twist on the more common male gladiator combats.[51]

Regardless, the *gladiatrix* battles continued until around 200 A.D., when the emperor Septimius Severus banned upper-class female gladiators seemingly because of the backlash directed towards all elite women. The ancient writer Cassius Dio wrote, "The women in this contest fought so energetically and savagely, that they were the cause of other elite women becoming the object of jokes and as a result, it was decreed that no woman should ever again fight in a gladiatorial duel."[52] After that decree, there are no shows that record the participation of female gladiators, upper-class or otherwise. This does not necessarily mean women ceased to compete in the arena, but it does at least suggest women fought less frequently.[53]

The *Hoplomachus*

---

[51] Dunkle (2008) pp.118-123, Shadrake (2005) pp.185-195 & Nossov (2009) pp.148-149. Dwarf vs. female combat: Cassius Dio, 67.8.4.
[52] Cassius Dio, 75.16.1.
[53] Dunkle (2008) pp.118-123, Shadrake (2005) pp.185-195 & Nossov (2009) pp.148-149.

A *hoplomachus* fighting a *thraex*

The name of this gladiator comes from Greek and means "fighting with weapons". Naturally, this gladiator class refers to the famous Greek hoplite warriors, who carried a shield called the *hoplon*, and this gladiator class was better known in the western part of the Roman Empire. The *hoplomachus* occasionally fought against the *thraex* gladiator, but he was more commonly paired against a *murmillo* fighter (though this latter pairing was much less common than the *murmillo* fighting the *thraex*).[54]

The *hoplomachus* was equipped with a helmet, shield, greaves and an armguard on his right arm. The helmet was broad-brimmed with a visor, and it was decorated with a forward curving crest and a feather, which could be placed on either side. Thus, this helmet closely resembled the helmet of the *thraex* gladiator. The shield was small, concave and rounded, made of a single sheet of metal (usually bronze), and looked much like the Greek hoplite shield. The back of the shield also had a broad bronze strip along the center, forming a stirrup where the fighter could place his lower arm. He could then grasp a leather loop fitted to the border of the shield.

As with the Greek hoplites, the structure of the *hoplomachus* shield allowed the gladiator to hold a dagger or short sword as his secondary weapon. His primary weapon was a lance, but if it was broken, lost or discarded, the *hoplomachus* could easily transfer his secondary weapon to his right hand. Presumably, the lance was used and discarded quickly because it would not have been a great one-handed offensive weapon.

Since this gladiator type only wore a loincloth with an accompanying belt and nothing on his torso, along with a small shield that did not offer much protection for his legs, this gladiator wore greaves on each leg that both reached as high as the middle of his thigh. Under them was cloth padding, which helped cover the upper part of the thigh and made the greaves more comfortable

---

[54] Junkelmann (2000) pp.51-57, Nossov (2009) pp.54-56 & Shadrake (2005) pp.160-162.

to wear. Based on images, the padding could be decorated with embroidery.[55]

Ancient art depicting a *thraex* fighting a kneeling *hoplomachus*
The *Laquearius*
The word *laquearius* means "lasso man", and hence his primary weapon was a lasso. It is unclear whether these gladiators were serious combatants or whether they were a novelty act like the *paegniarius*. Some even believe that this gladiator was a variety of the *retiarius*, carrying a lasso rather than a net, along with a short spear or dagger. Historian Roger Dunkle suggests that this gladiator fought like the modern day rodeo cowboy, except on foot, ensnaring his opponent, throwing him down and then possibly trying to strangle him. It is unclear what gladiator type he fought against, whether in serious combat or in jest, but it was probably another *laquearius*.[56]
The *Murmillo*

---

[55] Nossov (2009) pp.54-56, Dunkle (2008) p.104, Junkelmann (2000) pp.51-57 & Shadrake (2005) pp.160-162.
[56] Dunkle (2008) p.114, Junkelmann (2000) p.63, Nossov (2009) p.72 & Shadrake (2005) p.182.

A *murmillo* on the left trying to stab a *thraex* on the right

The name of this gladiator is frequently associated with the sea fish called *mormylos*, the image of which is occasionally found on his helmet. Given the name, this class of gladiator is often incorrectly thought to have fought against the *retiarius*, who was armed with a net.

The *murmillo* class began around the mid-1st century B.C., and it is believed that this type evolved from either the *samnis* or *gallus* gladiator of the Republican period. This gladiator never fought against his own class; instead, he was typically paired against someone with a smaller shield, like a *thraex* or *hoplomachus*. The most common pairing in the Imperial period was against the *thraex* gladiator, and these combats seem to have been very popular among the crowds. In fact, rivalries between fans of these two gladiator types are known to have occurred. In one famous example, because the Emperor Domitian's favorite gladiator was the *murmillo*, one literary source reports that he once threw a man to the dogs for speaking favorably about a *thraex* gladiator.[57]

The *murmillo* was equipped with a helmet, shield, armguard and greave. The helmet was made of bronze and had a broad brim with a bulging face plate, as well as a prominent visor and grillwork eye-pieces. On top of the helmet was a crest, often described as a huge fish dorsal fin, which usually had a plume made of feathers or horsehair. On either side of this plume there was a feather.

The *murmillo* wore only one greave on the left leg, which came up to just below the knee and

---

[57] Nossov (2009) pp.58-60, Dunkle (2008) pp.104-107, Junkelmann (2000) pp.48-51 & Shadrake (2005) pp.164-170. Domitian and the dogs: Suetonius, *Domitian*.4.2.

the lower part of the greave had a deep U-shaped cut, perhaps to better accommodate the cloth padding behind it. The right leg was protected by cloth padding or sometimes nothing. The right arm was equipped with an armguard, while the left arm was protected by his shield. The shield of the *murmillo* was large enough to protect the gladiator from his neck to the top of his greave, and may have weighed 13-25 pounds. Originally oval, it eventually became rectangular.

The *murmillo* gladiator did not wear any armor on his torso; the only item of clothing was a loincloth held up by an ornate belt. This gladiator class fought with a straight sword that was 40-55 centimeters long, and since it was their only weapon, it was often tied to his hand so that it was not lost during battle.[58]

The *Paegniarius*

The meaning of this gladiator is something like "play gladiator", and thus they are believed to have been used as comedic fighters in bouts that took place during the intervals between the deadly gladiatorial combats as light entertainment for the spectators. A 3rd century A.D. mosaic, believed to be of two *paegniarii* gladiators shows that they were only armed with non-lethal weapons, such as sticks and whips. Furthermore, they do not wear armor or helmets but are both entirely clothed, with their left arms shielded by either thick padding or perhaps some type of metal. In other words, by mimicking the movements of the more serious gladiators, the *paegniarii* would at most sustain bruises and small cuts.

Additionally, it is apparent they were primarily used for entertainment because the notoriously psychotic Roman emperor Caligula once forced upper class family members with physical disabilities to perform in place of the *paegniarii*. The inexperience and disability of the upper class men would have assuredly created a farcical image in the arena for the Roman spectators.

Regardless of the role of this gladiator class, they were still considered real gladiators. An inscription on the grave of a *paegniarius* named Secundus states that he belonged to the *Ludus Magnus*, the great imperial gladiatorial school located right next to the Colosseum.[59]

The *Provocator*

---

[58] Nossov (2009) pp.58-60, Dunkle (2008) pp.104-107, Junkelmann (2000) pp.48-51 & Shadrake (2005) pp.164-170.
[59] Dunkle (2008) pp.115-116, Shadrake (2005) pp.182-183, Junkelmann (2000) p.63 & Nossov (2009) pp.72-73. Suetonius, Caligula,26.5. *ILS* 5126.

Ancient depiction of a *provocator*

The *provocator* gladiator first appeared in the late 1st century B.C. during the Roman Republican period. The name of this gladiator means "challenger", referring to the manner in which he fought, which was to feign retreat and then attack quickly. It is also possible that the name of the gladiator comes from the Latin legal word *provocatio*, which referred to the right of appeal a condemned prisoner was given. Because of this, some argue that *provocatores* were originally criminals or prisoners of war who were sent to the arena, and if they fought well they could be given mercy. Another suggestion regarding *provocatores* was that they were retired Roman soldiers, a belief based on the fact that they were equipped like a Roman soldier. One of the earliest artistic representations of a *provocator* comes from a relief on a funeral monument. The two *provocatores* in this image wear loincloths, each with a wide ornate belt and an arm guard on the lower right arm that may have been metal or cloth padding. Each man is wearing a greave that extends just above the knee of the left leg and wears a breastplate held in place by leather straps over the shoulders and across the back. The *provocator* was the only gladiator that ever wore a chest protector, and thus it is one of the identifying features of this class.

The helmet was another identifying element of this gladiator type because it resembled that of the Roman legionnaire, with some slight alterations. The helmet in the image shows that it had wide cheek pieces and the brim at the back was extended to protect the neck. There was no crest on the helmet, but on each side was a feather. Each gladiator in the image had a different shield, one oval and the other rectangular, but both were used by the Roman military at that time. The *provocator* shield typically did not have an oval boss on the front, but rather only a vertical rib, and it was smaller than that of the *murmillo* shield. Both men were armed with a sword, the usual weapon for gladiators.

During the Imperial period, the *provocator* looked relatively the same except for changes to the helmet. The cheek guards disappeared, and a visor with round grillwork eyeholes became the new features. Other changes included increasing the size of the brim on the back and the sides in order to provide more protection for the neck. The rest of the equipment did not change from that of the Republican *provocator*. This gladiator only fought gladiators from the same class, although there must have been exceptions, as the inscription mentioning a battle between a *murmillo* and *provocator* indicates.[60]

The *Retiarius*

A retiarius trying to stab a secutor with his trident

This gladiator type is the easiest to recognize in Roman art due to his lack of shield and helmet, as well as the weapons he carried. While just about every other class resembled actual soldiers with heavy armor or weaponry, the *retiarius*, or "net-man", was equipped like a fisherman. It is unclear how the *retiarius* came into existence as there are no precedents for it, leading many to assume this type may have been created as an imaginative way to increase entertainment in the arena.

The *retiarius* began to appear in the 1st century A.D. and was primarily paired against the *secutor* gladiator. Although they were also known to have fought against a *murmillo* and *arbelas*, this was much less common, because the *retiarius* and *secutor* combination became very popular in the Roman world and remained so until the end of the gladiatorial games altogether. At the same time, according to at least some Roman literary, sources the *retiarius* was the least popular gladiator. This may be due to the fact that he was not equipped like the traditional Roman soldier and therefore had to apply tactics that were considered foreign. The Roman poet Juvenal shows

---

[60] Shadrake (2005) pp.147-149, Junkelmann (2000) pp.57-59, Dunkle (2008) p.101 & Nossov (2009) pp.61-62.

his disgust with this gladiator type in his treatise: "Beyond this, what is there, except the gladiatorial school? And that's where you've got the disgrace of Rome: a Gracchus fighting, but not in a *murmillo's* gear, and not with shield or curving blade. He rejects that sort of get-up, you see: look, he's brandishing a trident. Once he has poised his right hand and cast the trailing net without success, he raises his bare face to the spectators and runs off, highly recognisable, all through the arena. We can not mistake the tunic, since the ribbon of gold reaches from his neck, and flutters in the breeze from his high-peaked cap. Therefore, the disgrace, which the Secutor had to submit to, in being forced to fight with Gracchus, was worse than any wound."[61] In another passage, Juvenal notes, "So even the lanista's establishment is better ordered than yours, for he separates the vile from the decent, and sequesters even from their fellow-*retiarii* the wearers of the ill-famed tunic; in the training-school, and even in gaol, such creatures herd apart…"

A mosaic depicting a *retiarius* surrendering, with his net missing and the trident on the ground next to the *secutor*

As Juvenal's description suggests, the *retiarius* usually wore nothing except a loincloth and belt. His left arm was protected by an arm guard, and at the top was a *galerus* (shoulder guard) attached to the *manica*. The *galerus* was a square piece of bronze that had two pairs of loops on the inside so that it could be fastened to the arm. This guard projected 12-13 centimeters above the shoulder and was meant to offer protection for the neck and head, thus compensating for the lack of helmet. The upper rim of the *galerus* was also normally bent outward to slow sword blows directed towards the head. In the second and third centuries AD, in the eastern half of the Empire, images suggest that some of the *retiarius* gladiators substituted the *galerus* for armor that protected the left shoulder and part of the chest.

---

[61] Juvenal, *Satirae*, VIII.199-208. Taken from Shadrake (2005) p.175.

The weapons of this gladiator type were the net, dagger and trident, a set of equipment that all but ensured the *retiarii's* unusual fighting style. The net was presumably the first weapon used, as the *retiarius* tried to tangle the *secutor*. If this failed, the *retiarius* was left with his dagger and trident, with the latter being the more effective weapon because it could parry sword thrusts while still having an effective reach for attacks. The trident, which was about the height of a man, was even more effective if held with both hands, as the thrusts would have been heavier and more destructive. The dagger was the least dangerous weapon and was probably used as a last resort or if the *retiarius* was forced to engage in close combat. Of course, due to the lack of protective armor or shield, however, the *retiarius* probably tried to avoid close combat.[62]

This mosaic depicts a *retiarius* named Kalendio fighting a *secutor* named Astyanax. Astyanax is stuck in Kalendio's net in the lower image, but in the top image, Kalendio is on the ground raising his arm to surrender.

The *Sagittarius*
The *sagittarius* means "archer" or "shooter", an indication that this gladiator type fought with the bow and arrow, but the literary and archaeological sources are scarce concerning the appearance of this gladiator class. The few images that do exist show that the *sagittarius* gladiator was armed with a composite bow, pointed helmet and scale armor. They also appear to

---
[62] Nossov (2009) pp.62-66, Dunkle (2008) pp.107-111, Shadrake (2005) pp.173-182 & Junkelmann (2000) pp.59-61.

have fought gladiators of the same type. When these kinds of combats occurred within the arena, extra safety precautions assuredly had to be taken because the bows could fire arrows over 600 feet, meaning an arrow that missed its mark could find its way into the audience. Well-armored soldiers likely watched the action closely and were there to help protect the spectators from being inadvertently hit by an arrow from one of the gladiators.[63]

The *Samnis*

The *samnis* gladiator was named after the warriors of the Samnite tribe in Italy defeated by Rome in the 3rd century B.C.. The 1st century B.C. Roman historian Livy described the Samnite warriors: "The Samnites, besides their other warlike preparations, had made their battle line to glitter with new and splendid arms. There were two corps: the shields of the one were inlaid with gold and the shields of the other with silver. The shape of the shield was this: the upper part, where it protected the breast and shoulders, was rather broad with a level top; below it was somewhat tapering, to make it easier to handle. They wore a *spongia* (ring mail?) to protect the breast and the left leg was covered with a greave. Their helmets were crested, to make their stature appear greater."[64]

Historians are unsure what to make of Livy's description of Samnite warriors because the archaeological evidence seems to be at odds with his account, and it is therefore presumed that Livy is actually describing the appearance of the *samnis* gladiator. When the *samnis* actually became a specific gladiator type is uncertain, but they were a gladiator category by at least the end of the 2nd century B.C., and by then the *samnis* probably no longer looked like an authentic Samnite warrior. Instead, based on surviving images, the *samnis* gladiator wore a wide-brimmed helmet with a ridge of feathers, one greave on his left leg and possibly chest armor with three discs on the breast plate. Shadrake believes that the right arm was protected by some type of armor but the torso was not. The *samnis* gladiator was armed with a sword and/or spear and carried a large oval or rectangular shield. This class of gladiator was only around during the Republican period and may have influenced the appearance of the *murmillo* and *secutor* gladiators of the Imperial period.[65]

The *Secutor/contraretiarius*

---

[63] Nossov (2009) p.74, Dunkle (2008) pp.116-117 & Junkelmann (2000) pp.63-64.
[64] Livy, 9.40.2-3. Taken from Shadrake (2005) pp.132-133.
[65] Shadrake (2005) pp.132-142, Junkelmann (2000) p.37 & Nossov (2009) pp.74-75.

Figurine of a secutor

The *secutor* gladiator was created specifically to fight against the *retiarius* and also first appeared in the mid-1st century A.D. The ancient historian Suetonius mentioned the *secutores* fighting against their main adversaries, the *retiarii*, writing: "Five *retiarii*, in tunics, fighting in a company, yielded without a struggle to the same number of opponents; and being ordered to be slain, one of them taking up his trident again, killed all the conquerors." *Secutor* means "chaser" or "pursuer", and this class is similar to that of the *murmillo* type in every way except for the helmet.

This gladiator class was protected by a large rectangular shield, a greave on his left leg and an arm guard on his right arm. He was also armed with a sword. The *secutor* helmet was specifically designed with his opponent the *retiarius* in mind. As he fought only against the *retiarius*, the *secutor* had to ensure his helmet was not caught up in his opponent's net or pierced too easily by the trident. Therefore the *secutor* helmet was smooth with no decoration except for a crest on top, which may have been sharp. This design ensured that the net of the *retiarius* could not catch anything on the helmet. The back of the helmet curled slightly outward to protect the neck, and the face plate only had two very small eyeholes. The eyeholes were smaller than those on other gladiator helmets in order to prevent the points of the trident from piercing through too easily. The *secutor* was forced to engage in close combat because of the limitations the helmet created, such as decreased vision, hearing and access to fresh air. Therefore this gladiator had to be cautious not to waste too much energy fighting against the much faster moving but less protected *retiarius*. The overall result was a more even match between these two opponents.[66]

The *Thraex*/Thracian

A flask depicts a *murmillo* defeating a *thraex*

In the 1st century B.C., the famous dictator Sulla was the first person to introduce the *thraex* gladiator, named and after the conquered Thracians from the territory that is now known as

---

[66] Nossov (2009) p.67, Dunkle (2008) pp.112-113, Shadrake (2005) pp.171-172 & Junkelmann (2000) pp.61-63. Suetonius, *Caligula*.30.3, taken from Nossov (2009) p.67.

Bulgaria. The most famous *thraex* gladiator was Spartacus, who later led a slave rebellion against the Romans, and like Spartacus, the original *thraex* gladiators were probably actual Thracian warriors. However, over time a *thraex* gladiator was likely just a gladiator who appeared in the arena brandishing similar weapons and armor and did not actually have to be from the region of Thrace. It is difficult to determine with any certainty exactly how the early *thraex* gladiator appeared, but they were probably armed with the short, curved, dagger-like blade called the *sica*, and wore a helmet similar to that of a Roman soldier.

Unlike the other ethnically named gladiators from the Republican period, the *thraex* gladiator was so popular it continued into the Imperial period, and it is this period that produced most of the information as to how this type was equipped. The *thraex* carried a small convex square or rectangular shield measuring 55x60 centimeters, and since this was a small shield, this gladiator required much more protection on his body. Therefore, he also wore a greave on both legs that went up to mid-thigh, with cloth padding underneath rising all the way up to the groin. He also wore an arm guard on the right arm, which may have been cloth padding or metal. Lastly the *thraex* wore a helmet, which was usually quite identifiable by the distinctive griffin's head on the crest. The crest could also be plumed with feathers, as well as have feathers on either side of the helmet. Like the helmets of the *murmillo* and *hoplomachus*, it had a prominent visor with grillwork eye-pieces. This gladiator was believed to have been armed with the customary curved *sica*, just as his Republican counterpart, and in the arena, the *thraex* was traditionally paired against either the *murmillo* or the *hoplomachus* gladiator.[67]

The *Veles*

This class of gladiator takes its name from the lightly armed foot soldiers of the Roman Republican period, who were skirmishers called *velites*. As soldiers, the *velites* carried a short javelin, a sword and shield. They ceased to be a part of the Roman army by the late Republican period, but they appear in literary sources as gladiators until the end of the 2nd century B.C. Literary sources, artwork and archaeological evidence are scarce regarding how the *veles* gladiator was equipped, but it is believed that the *veles* was armed with a spear that had a strap, which may have been used to help throw it. This gladiator may have also had a sword and shield, as did his soldier counterpart, but this is unclear. There is no evidence suggesting whether or not these gladiators wore any armor, and it is thought that they likely just wore a tunic and a leather cap. The *veles* only fought against others from the same gladiator class, and the combat probably entailed tossing spears at one another.[68]

The Gladiators' Equipment

"[W]eapons training was given to soldiers by P. Rutilius, consul with C. Mallis. For he, following the example of no previous general, with teachers summoned from the gladiatorial training school of C. Aurelus Scaurus, implanted in the legions a more sophisticated method of avoiding and dealing a blow and mixed bravery with skill and skill back again with virtue so that skill became stronger by bravery's passion and passion became more wary with the knowledge of this art." – Valerius Maximus

The majority of information regarding gladiator equipment comes from archaeological sources, particularly the gladiatorial barracks in the Roman city of Pompeii, which was famously buried (and thus preserved) by Mount Vesuvius' eruption in the late 1st century A.D. Another important source for understanding the evolution of gladiator equipment comes from artwork, which can be

---

[67] Shadrake (2005) pp.143-146 & 155-160, Nossov (2009) pp.68-69, Dunkle (2008) pp.101-104 & Junkelmann (2000) pp.51-57.
[68] Dunkle (2008) p.113, Shadrake (2005) p.154 & Nossov (2009) pp.77-78.

quite informative other than those occasions where the artwork is damaged or does not clearly show the details of the equipment. The literary sources are not as valuable because the descriptions are typically pretty general or there is no description of the equipment at all.

Art depicting the amphitheater and gladiators inside the arena in Pompeii

One important element of the gladiatorial equipment that has been found is that much of it is decorated with ornate reliefs. This has created a debate on whether decorated equipment was functional or ceremonial. An argument for a ceremonial purpose is that decorations decreased the sturdiness of the metal, making it more fragile as a protective piece of armor. In addition to that problem, equipment adorned with reliefs would have been heavier, as more metal is needed for the ornate designs, making the equipment that much less practical. Ornate equipment would be more expensive to make, so gladiators and lanistas would theoretically not want it damaged, a theory corroborated by the fact that the surviving examples of decorative gladiator equipment rarely have any damage, suggesting that it was never used in actual combat..

Regardless of these arguments, there are those who believe that richly designed armor was in fact used in the arena. Those who believe decorative equipment was used argue that it was not expensive because the equipment was likely shared by more than one man, so not as many ornate pieces of armor were necessary. Concerning the weight of the equipment, many believe that since the armor was only worn for a short period of time, the extra weight was likely insignificant. As for lack of damage, these proponents note that gladiators typically used light short swords in the arena, not heavy slashing instruments, and the light swords were not strong enough to cut through armor, whether it was decorative or not. However, the biggest piece of evidence that gladiators wore decorative armor is that artistic representations clearly show gladiators wearing ornate equipment.[69]

The early helmets worn by gladiators in the Roman Republican period in the 1st century B.C. were similar to those of Roman soldiers. They had a broad, bent-down brim, a forehead plate and wide cheek-guards fastened on hinges. However, by the Imperial period and the 1st century A.D., the gladiator's helmet moved away from the military helmet in a variety of ways depending on the gladiator class. The gladiators belonging to the *murmillo*, *thraex*, *hoplomachus* and *eques* classes had a helmet that evolved into two different types that were distinguished by the shape of the brim. One type had a horizontal brim that went around the entire helmet, while the other one had a horizontal brim at the back and on the sides, and at the front it went sharply up over the forehead creating a peak. This latter helmet would transition into another type that began to appear around the middle of the 2nd century A.D., which was characterized by a very low brim at the back and the sides and then a nearly vertical brim at the front, practically framing the visor of the helmet. This did not mean that the older helmet styles ceased to exist, only that by the 3rd century A.D. there were three different types of helmets that could be worn by gladiators.

Most gladiator helmets had a visor, which obscured the appearance of the gladiator and thus made him anonymous, with the exception of the *retiarius*, who wore no helmet at all. The visor was made of two hinged metal halves that opened horizontally and met at the front, where there was a metal rib placed to protect the spot where they joined. The visor was fastened by metal latches either at the top or the bottom, and the lower half of the visor was kept in place with help from a leather strap and the metal. The bottom was bent outwards to protect the throat. The hinges were vulnerable and could break easily, so they were protected themselves by plates, which additionally strengthened the visor. The earliest gladiator helmets had round apertures for the eyes measuring around 8 centimeters in diameter and were often screened with grating-plates to help protect the eyes, but by the end of the 1st century A.D. all visors had a metal grate covering the upper portion of the face while the lower parts remained solid metal. This grating opened similarly to the earlier versions but closely followed the contours of the helmet's brim.

The helmet was also different for the *secutor*, *arbelas*, *provocator* and *essedarius* gladiators. The *secutor* and *arbelas* helmet never had a brim or a grating visor; instead, the apertures for the eyes were only 3 centimeters in diameter and were never covered with grating. However, in the 2nd century A.D. the visor of some *secutor* helmets were dotted with small openings, perhaps to help with breathing or to increase the field of vision (or both). In some parts of the Roman Empire, artwork shows that the *secutor* helmet by the 3rd century A.D. may have had a crest that went from the back of the head to the chin, and it may or may not have been sharp. Another interesting fact about the *secutor* helmet was that it was thicker than most other gladiator helmets. Historian Marcus Junkelmann believes this is due to the fact that the trident of the *retiarius* could severely damage a helmet if used by two hands.

---

[69] Junkelmann (2000) pp.38-45 & Nossov (2009) pp.80-83.

The early *provocator* helmet was modeled after that of the Roman soldier, with cheek guards but no visor. However, during the 1st century A.D. this helmet acquired a forehead plate and a visor with eye holes that could be covered with gratings. The *essedarius* helmet was also originally similar to that of Roman soldiers, but by the middle of the 1st century A.D. this helmet closely resembled that of the *secutor* helmet. The major difference between the two was that rather than having a crest, the *essedarius* helmet had a feather on each side.

Although they're common in depictions of gladiators today, not every gladiator type had a crest on top of the helmet. Only the *murmillo*, *thraex*, *hoplomachus*, *arbelas* and *secutor* helmets had crests, and they were all unique from one another. The *murmillo* crest, believed to resemble a dorsal fin, rose vertically in the back, bent 90 degrees and then went horizontally towards the front, with a groove at the top that allowed for feathers or horsehair to be affixed. Meanwhile, the crest of the *thraex* helmet curved from the back towards the front and ended with a griffin's head that could be crowned with feathers. The *hoplomachus* helmet had a crest as well, which, according to artwork, resembled the *thraex* helmet minus the griffin design. That said, unfortunately, no surviving example has been found, so the exact shape remains elusive. The *arbelas* and *secutor* helmets both had a narrow crest with no plumes whatsoever, the only two helmets that did not seem to ever have feathers placed on either side of the helmet.

Most helmets were made of bronze, but the surface could be silvered or tinned, and once polished they would have gleamed in the sun during conflict. Whether they were decorated any further remains unknown. Presumably, either the inside of the helmet was padded or the gladiator wore some type of cloth hat, because otherwise any impact would have easily been felt. Although the helmets weighed approximately 7-11 pounds, making them quite heavy, it is presumed that since contests lasted on average perhaps 15 minutes, the weight of the helmet would not have been too problematic for the fighter.[70]

The gladiators' arm guard (*manica*) was derived from the *caestus* (a boxing glove), meaning it was originally short and protected probably only the hand and perhaps the elbow. Eventually it was extended to the shoulder, though technically shorter ones could still be worn, and for the most part every gladiator wore an arm guard on their right arm unless they were left handed. The exception to this was the *retiarius*, who wore his on the left arm. Gladiators equipped with small shields could wear an arm guard on both arms. The earliest *manica* was made of multi-layered cloth or leather that wrapped around the entire arm and was held on with leather straps. The hand and thumb were only covered on the outside, but a leather loop went across the fingers to secure it. Although originally not made of metal, the cloth or leather arm guard could adequately protect the arm from slashing blows, while still providing good mobility at the joints. Only direct thrusts would cause immediate damage and harm to the arm.

---

[70] Nossov (2009) pp.82-90, Shadrake (2005) pp.171-172 & Junkelmann (2000) pp.38-45.

The Roman soldier's manica is clearly visible in this art

In the second century AD, the *manica* was made of metal. One drawback to this, however, was that the mobility of the arm was greatly lessened. This problem was fixed when a detached elbow-protecting plate was created. It is probable that a light cloth wrapping was still worn underneath the metal to decrease friction and give the gladiator some comfort. Although the metal *manica* was preferred, there is pictorial evidence showing that the multi-layered cloth and leather arm guard continued to be used. The choice of arm guard may have depended on personal preference with each gladiator taking into account which type was more comfortable, provided better mobility, and other factors such as whether or not he was already adequately equipped with armor and a large shield.[71]

The *ocrea*, or greave, was influenced by the Greek hoplites who wore it. Unlike the gladiator greaves, however, the hoplite greaves wrapped around the entire leg and required no straps to

---

[71] Nossov (2009) pp.90-91 & Shadrake (2005) pp.195-204.

secure them on, whereas those worn by gladiators protected only the shin and a little bit on the sides and were kept on with straps passed through two to four rings. The gladiator greave was a single piece of bronze, which could be plain or decorated, and fabric was normally worn under the greaves both for additional protection as well as a lining between the metal and skin. Many of the surviving greaves have inscriptions on them, which may indicate which gladiatorial school the greaves were made at.

The size of the greaves varied depending on the type of gladiator. Some greaves just covered the shin, some came to just below the knee, and others went past the knee. Each size had distinctive characteristics too; the shorter greaves had a U-shaped cut at the bottom, while greaves that covered the knee had a projection for the kneecap. Furthermore, the length of the shield may have also determined the design of the greaves. For example, the greaves of the *murmillo* and *secutor* had a bend at the top presumably to protect their legs from being hit by their larger shields, while some gladiators, such as the *essedarius* and *retiarius*, did not have shields and thus did not wear any greaves. The number of greaves a gladiator wore, whether one or two, was dependent on gladiator type.[72]

The first gladiator shields were modeled on those of the Roman army and subsequently changed as the army changed theirs. Originally oval, by the mid-1st century A.D. they mostly became rectangular with sides bent inward. This type of shield was made from two or three layers of wood glued perpendicular to one another, and on the outside, it was covered with leather or felt and edged with bronze or iron strips. A wooden strip ran down the entire shield, which provided additional strength, and in the center of the outer section was a bronze or iron oval boss to help deflect blows. The outer surface was then covered with a decorative ornament. The shape and size of the shield depended on the type of gladiator, but the only shield carrying gladiator who did not use this wooden shield was the *hoplomachus*, who used a bronze shield. The bronze shields could be flat or slightly bulging and sometimes had alternating concentric circles of stiffening ribs and grooves.

The size of gladiator shields often created rivalries between fans, with some favoring the larger shield and others liking the smaller shield. Fans of gladiators carrying a large shield (called a *scutum*) were called the *scutarii*, while fans of the smaller shield (called the *parma*) were called *parmularii*. Typically, this rivalry focused on the *murmillo* and the *thraex* pairing because the *murmillo* carried a *scutum* and the latter was equipped with the *parma*. Even emperors had their favorites and occasionally punished those favoring the opposition. For example, Domitian would sometimes send *parmularii* to death by fire in the arena simply because they spoke out against the *scutum*.[73]

The outfit for many of the gladiators normally consisted of a loincloth and a belt. The belt was fairly wide, measuring 8-12 centimeters. Made of bronze and resting on a lining of leather, it was fastened with two hooks at the back. By the Late Empire (3rd century A.D.) the belt changed and some gladiators began to wear a belt of ring-clasps. With the torso bare, the chest became an area of the body open to attack and made any wounds that were incurred visible for all spectators to see. Furthermore, the bare chest allowed spectators, particularly women, to see the rippling muscles of the men. Gladiators were also typically barefoot and the leg not protected by a greave often had a leather strap with tassels tied around it. The tassels may have signified the number of wins for the gladiator, but this is pure speculation. Some gladiators, such as the *eques*, and

---

[72] Shadrake (2005) pp.204-208 & Nossov (2009) pp.91-94.
[73] Shadrake (2005) pp.165-167, Nossov (2009) pp.95-98 & Dunkle (2008) pp.106-107. Pliny the Younger, *Pan*.33.3-4.

occasionally the *retiarius*, are shown wearing a tunic, while others, such as the *arbelas*, *crupellarius* and *dimachaerus*, who did not carry a shield, are depicted wearing some type of armor. These latter gladiators may in fact be wearing tunics rather than metal, but the evidence is not clear enough to determine with certainty.[74]

When gladiatorial combat first began in the Republican period the weapon used was primarily the spear. However, it became rarer by the 1st century B.C., except in the hands of a few gladiator types like the *hoplomachus*, *eques*, *venator* and *essedarius*. Surviving spearheads indicate they were made of bronze and had a socket where the wooden pole was inserted.

By the 2nd century B.C., the primary weapon for gladiators was the Spanish sword, which not coincidentally also happened to be the main weapon of Roman soldiers. This weapon was a straight, broad, double-edged sword with a longitudinal stiffening rib and clearly marked point, measuring approximately 65 centimeters. The blade was most broad near the handle, narrowed slightly and then widened again. The handle could be made entirely of wood, ivory, or some combination of the two.

The Spanish sword was great for thrusting, but by the mid-1st century A.D. it was eventually supplanted by another weapon called the Pompeii sword. This was a shorter and narrower double-edged blade that turned 45 degrees as it reached towards the point. When the sword of the Roman infantry became longer in the 2nd and 3rd centuries A.D., measuring around 75 centimeters, the swords of gladiators followed suit. The other main weapon, primarily used by the *retiarius* and *hoplomachus* gladiator, was the dagger. This straight bladed weapon began appearing more frequently around the 1st century A.D. and was used for thrusting in close combat against opponents.

Although the sword and dagger were the most common weapons, they were not the only ones. Two other weapons of the *retiarius* gladiator were the net and trident. Based on surviving images, the net was round, 3 to 4 meters in diameter, and containing 20-30 centimeter wide cells. It is possible that there were also small lead weights sewed along the perimeter of the net in order for it to fly further when tossed.

---

[74] Shadrake (2005) pp.168-170 & 210-211 & Nossov (2009) pp.101-102.

The Day of the Show

A mosaic depicting different kinds of events held in Roman amphitheatres

"For death, when it stands near us, gives even to inexperienced men the courage not to seek to avoid the inevitable. So the gladiator, no matter how faint-hearted he has been throughout the fight, offers his throat to his opponent and directs the wavering blade to the vital spot." - Seneca

Gladiators (literally, "swordsmen") were the superstar athletes of the Roman world, and the Romans were so fond of gladiatorial combat that they constructed mammoth arenas in which to witness their heroes do battle, the most famous being the 50,000 seat Colosseum, which still eclipses many modern sports stadiums in size. Gladiators could aspire to undying fame, fortune, riches, and the favors of as many women, both high-born and lowborn, as they could wish for. Their portraits would be graffitied onto city walls, and effigies of them would be sold by traders in markets. Given the possibility of both glory and great rewards, many men were tempted by the gladiator's life, which is why their ranks contained not just slaves but freedmen (ex-slaves who lacked social mobility) and even Roman citizens who had volunteered despite the danger.

Gladiatorial contests could involve fights against animals or, as the demand for spectacle grew, all-out battles, but the most popular type of spectacle remained the one-on-one combat, which was the province of professional gladiators. Unfair fights against overwhelming numbers of beasts, often with inappropriate weaponry, were left to condemned criminals, religious dissidents, and escaped slaves. The Romans considered those spectacles to be comical more than anything else, but they fully appreciated a fight among gladiators themselves.

Most people associate the arena with gladiatorial combat, and while gladiators did fight in the Roman amphitheatre, much more happened within the arena on a typical day. In fact, Romans attending spectacles at the Colosseum or a similar amphitheatre could expect a specific schedule of events. The morning entailed spectacles involving animals (*venationes*), followed by public executions during the lunch break. Of course, the best was saved for last, with gladiatorial combats commencing in the afternoon. Thus, a day at the amphitheatre offered various forms of entertainment, not merely one kind of event or contest.[75]

A typical Roman show (*munus*) began with a *pompa*, which was a procession or parade. The organizer of the games entered the arena first accompanied by musicians, *lictors* (Roman magistrates), and people carrying tablets that informed the audience of the day's events. Lastly the gladiators, *venatores* (beast hunters) and condemned convicts entered the arena at the back of the *pompa*. Pliny the Elder once took note of the art promoting and advertising the gladiators and described it: "When a freedman of Nero was giving a gladiatorial show at Antium, the public porticoes were covered with paintings, so we are told, containing life-like portraits of all the gladiators and assistants. This portraiture of gladiators has been the highest interest in art for many centuries now, but it was Gaius Terentius who began the practice of having pictures made of gladiatorial shows and exhibited in public; in honour of his grandfather who had adopted him he provided thirty pairs of Gladiators in the Forum for three consecutive days, and exhibited a picture of the matches in the Grove of Diana."

After the procession concluded, the morning events began, which entailed a variety of animal shows, began. This included animal parades, hunts, animals battling one another and animals performing tricks. In order to make it more exciting, a carnivore would usually be pitted against an herbivore or another carnivore, and Martial described a couple of these encounters.

> "Wont to lick the hand of its fearless master, a tigress, sprung, their unmatched glory, from Hyrcanian hills, savagely tore a fierce lion with maddened fang: strange was the thing, unknown in any age! She ventured no such deed what time she dwelt in her deep woods: she is in our midst, and shows more fierceness now."[76]
>
> ...
>
> "While in fear the trainers were goading a rhinoceros, and long was the great beast's wrath gathering strength, all despaired of the conflict of the promised war; yet at length the fury, known erewhile, returned. For a heavy bear he tossed with his double horn, even as a bull hurls dummies heavenward, and with as sure an aim as that wherewith the stout right hand of Carpophorus, as yet young, levels the Noric hunting-spear. That beast, agile with pliant neck, stood up against a pair of steers, to him yielded the fierce buffalo and bison; a lion in flight from him ran headlong upon the spears. Go now, ye rabble, and gird at slow delays!"[77]

---
[75] Hopkins & Beard (2005) p.55.
[76] Martial, *Spectacles*.18.

In addition to animals being engaged with other animals, they could also be pitted against men. Professional hunters (*venatores*) fought against ferocious beasts or hunted non-vicious animals, such as deer or rabbits, and these hunters were accompanied by lower ranking attendants (*bestiarii*) who may have been responsible for bringing animals into the arena and then provoking them to fight if they did not cooperate. Although the audience expected the animals to be defeated, animals could be unpredictable, and hunters or their attendants were often be killed instead. Naturally, this unpredictability assuredly made the morning shows very entertaining to the Roman crowds.[78] Martial detailed a couple of these performances:

> "While on the bloody sand a bear whirled with lowered head, he lost the escape that bird-lime clogged. Let now the burnished hunting spears, their steel hidden, lie at rest, nor the lance fly hurled from projected arm; let the hunter take his prey in the empty air, if by the fowler's art one may catch beasts."[79]
>
> …
>
> "When, amid the cruel hazards of Caesar's hunt, a light spear had pierced a pregnant sow, there sprang forth one of her offspring from the wound of its unhappy dam."[80]

Lunch was designated for the execution of criminals and prisoners of war, and these condemned individuals were either crucified, burned alive, executed by gladiators, or had ferocious animals set upon them (*ad bestias*). Occasionally, the executions were turned into an even bigger spectacle by staging them as a mythological play in which the condemned individuals died at the end. Martial wrote about some of the mythical reenactments he witnessed within the Colosseum:[81]

> "That Pasiphae was mated to the Dictaean bull, believe: we have seen it, the old-time myth has won its warrant. And let not age-long old, Caesar, marvel at itself: whatever Fame sings of, that the Arena makes real for thee."[82]
>
> …
>
> "Daedalus, now thou art being so mangled by a Lucanian boar, how wouldst thou wish thou hadst now thy wings!"[83]
>
> …
>
> "Whereas the earth yawned suddenly and sent forth a she-bear to attack Orpheus, the bear came from Eurydice."[84]

---

[77] Martial, *Spectacles*.22.
[78] Köhne & Ewigleben (2000) pp.71-74.
[79] Martial, *Spectacles*.11.
[80] Martial, *Spectacles*.12.1-4.
[81] Hopkins & Beard (2005) pp.45-47.
[82] Martial, *Spectacles*.5.
[83] Martial, *Spectacles*.8.
[84] Martial, *Spectacles*.21b.

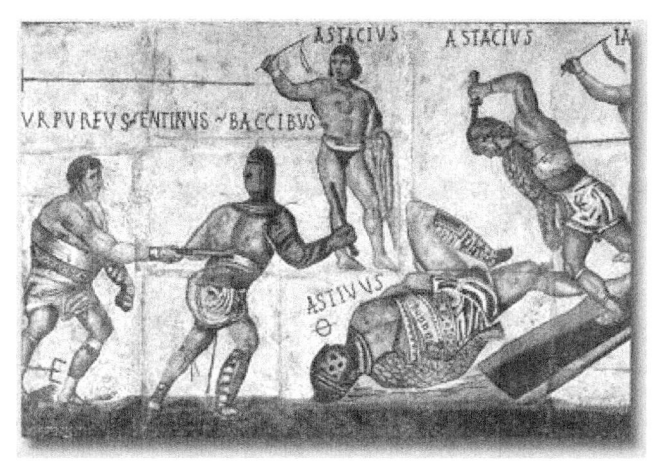

Depiction of gladiatorial combat from the Gladiator Mosaic (ca. 320 AD). The Ø symbol denotes that gladiator as being killed in combat.

The last spectacles of the day were the gladiatorial combats, and the first gladiator event involved a pair of combatants fighting with non-lethal weapons. The purpose of this event was for the gladiators to demonstrate their skills for the audience. Next came another display in which gladiators tested the variety of deadly weapons for the crowd. After these warm-up events, the main event - potentially lethal combats - would commence. Usually, each battle was between two gladiators fighting each other, but in a really big or special event, there might be teams of gladiators fighting each other.

When the battle began, the two gladiators would fight until there was a victor, but breaks could be given if both gladiators were exhausted or if the battle was becoming too long. Furthermore, there were two judges, an umpire and his assistant, who watched the combat to ensure that the rules were not broken. It is unfortunate that the actual rules of gladiatorial combats do not survive, but literary sources indicate that the umpire could strike the gladiators with his stick if the fighters were not following the rules or not putting up a suitable fighting effort. If this punishment failed, the assistant could use a whip, torch or red-hot iron. Although this probably happened, scholars assume that these punishments were used against the criminal gladiators rather than against the professional fighters themselves.

A match ended in one of three ways. The first was if one of the gladiators died, was mortally wounded or believed by the umpire to be unable to continue due to his wounds. The match could also end if a gladiator surrendered due to exhaustion or injury. When a gladiator surrendered, he extended his arm and raised a finger, upon which the umpire would stop the match, and the fate of this surrendering gladiator subsequently depended on the sponsor, who usually based his decision on the sentiment of the Roman crowd. If the gladiator had fought with skill, spirit, courage and valor, the audience may have wanted to spare his life. If dissatisfied, the audience would let the sponsor know and the gladiator would be executed. If the gladiator was not spared, he would still be expected to face his death honorably. He would place his hands on the ground or behind his back and await the final stroke. Lastly, a combat could end if both gladiators had fought for a long time. In this instance, if both of the fighters had impressed the crowd with their skill and determination, the match could be declared a draw.

A professional gladiator who was killed was usually carried away carefully from the arena and given a proper funeral, while criminal gladiators were dragged away with hooks. Meanwhile, any wounded gladiators were given proper medical care, as it was hoped they could be used again in future shows, thus providing more money for the *lanista*. The winning gladiator usually received an award, consisting of a palm branch and sometimes even money, and he would then make a lap around the arena, if capable, waving his palm branch at the crowd. A gladiator who had obtained a significant amount of victories could be given a wooden sword (*rudis*) as a prize, which signified that he no longer had to fight in the arena.[85]

Despite the constant danger of death, it appears as though being a gladiator, at least a professional one, was not as perilous as might initially appear. Evidence suggests that professional gladiators were not as likely to die as commonly believed, because fights, even if they were often nominally "to the death", frequently ended with a wound that might not necessarily be incapacitating. Since gladiators benefitted from the very best medical care available, provided by their *lanista*, they were often able to recover from wounds that might have otherwise proved mortal. Additionally, the Roman public was far less likely to show a defeated opponent the *pollice verso* ("turned thumb") than modern films and literature suggest, particularly because the man who had fallen might well be a beloved champion with a large following. For example, one gladiator's tombstone read, "Flamma, secutor, lived 30 years, fought 34 times, won 21 times, fought to a draw 9 times, defeated 4 times, a Syrian by nationality. Delicatus made this for his deserving comrade-in-arms."

Interestingly, scholars still debate to this day whether "thumbs up" signified the public's desire to spare an opponent or have him killed; although the common belief is that spectators would give a thumb-up or thumb-down sign to indicate their decision, there is no evidence to indicate exactly what the audience did to communicate their decision. Martial described how two gladiators once fought to a draw in the Colosseum:

> "While Priscus drew out, and Verus drew out the contest, and the prowess of both stood long in balance, oft was discharge for the men claimed with mighty shouts; but Caesar himself obeyed his own law: that law was, when the prize was set up, to fight until the finger was raised; what was lawful he did, oft giving dishes and gifts therein. Yet was an end found of that balanced strife: they fought well matched, matched well they together yielded. To each Caesar sent the wooden sword, and rewards to each this prize dexterous valour won. Under no prince but thee, Caesar, has this chanced: while two fought, each was victor."[86]

Another event that may have taken place in the Colosseum and involved men fighting was a sea battle (*naumachiae*), as ancient passages written by Martial and Cassius Dio both describe a sea battle taking place during the Colosseum's inauguration in 80 A.D. Martial wrote:

> "Whoever you are who come from distant shores, a late spectator, for whom this day of the sacred show is your first, that this naval battle with its ships, and the waters that represent seas, may not mislead, I tell you 'here but now was land.' Believe you not? Look on while the seas weary the God of war. Wait one moment-you will say 'Here but now was sea.'"[87]

---

[85] Junkelmann (2000) pp.64-69, Dunkle (2008) pp.72-78 & 94-97, Meijer (2004) pp.159-175 & Nossov (2009) pp.156-167.
[86] Martial, *Spectacles*.29.

Cassius Dio, writing in the 2d century A.D., corroborated Martial's account and provided more detail:

> "As for the men, several fought in single combat and several groups contended together both in infantry and naval battles. For Titus suddenly filled this same theatre with water and brought in horses and bulls and some other domesticated animals that had been taught to behave in the liquid element just as on land. He also brought in people on ships, who engaged in a sea-fight there, impersonating the Corcyreans and Corinthians; and others gave a similar exhibition outside the city in the grove of Gaius and Lucius, a place which Augustus had once excavated for this very purpose. There, too, on the first day there was a gladiatorial exhibition and wild-beast hunt, the lake in front of the images having first been covered over with a platform of planks and wooden stands erected around it."[88]

If the arena was ever actually flooded, it was probably before the reign of Domitian, since he was the one who began adding the subterranean galleries. In its present state, the arena could not possibly hold water for ships to battle one another, so if the event did occur in the Colosseum, the arena would not originally have had these subterranean galleries yet.[89]

A painting imagining a naumachia by Ulpiano Checa.

Even if gladiators weren't killed in combat as often as modern society thinks, there's still no

---

[87] Martial, *Spectacles*.24.
[88] Cassius Dio, 66.25.2-4.
[89] Kyle (1998) p.51 & Hopkins & Beard (2005) p.136-142. See also Suetonius, *Divus Titus*.7.

question that participation was incredibly hazardous. Since gladiators were so popular, the very first combats, which were designed to end with the loser dying, were quickly discarded so that the supply of gladiators was never too low. Nevertheless, historian George Ville estimated that a gladiator entering the arena had about a 20% chance of dying, so the odds were stacked against gladiators who fought in many matches. Studies done on gladiator cemeteries indicates most of them died before they were 30 years old, and chances were that they didn't make it to a 10th match alive. Furthermore, the rate of death seemed to rise over time, suggesting that fewer losing gladiators were spared. This makes sense given the proclivities of emperors like Caligula, whose thirst for blood often led him to refuse sparing losers that the crowds wanted to live.

It is difficult to determine the frequency with which spectacles were held in the Colosseum during the Roman Empire. The inaugural games in 80 A.D. were certainly one of the largest spectacles to take place there, as sources record that Titus had 100 days of games, during which thousands of animals were killed, many prisoners were executed, countless gladiators fought and even a sea battle was presented. Another large spectacle was given by the emperor Trajan over a period of 123 days, during which he had thousands of animals killed and had thousands of gladiator matches in order to commemorate his Dacian victories. These were two of the biggest, but other emperors were known to have held games, including Domitian, Commodus and Probus.

Besides the emperors, aristocrats could hold games in the Colosseum as well, but ancient sources rarely mention these spectacles because they were immensely scaled down compared to those given by the emperor. Aristocrats could not outshine the emperor, and in fact there was legislation limiting the total number of gladiators an aristocrat could present in any given show. Nevertheless, in order to mark public advancement or gain political support, aristocrats gave spectacles to the public, and on these occasions some were certainly held within the Colosseum.[90]

The Colosseum is still famous for the games it held, but it was also a place where Romans could confront the emperor. By the Flavian dynasty, Rome was strictly an authoritarian empire in which the people had little say in political matters, so the Colosseum was one place where the people could collectively confront the emperor on matters that concerned them. If there was something that disturbed the population, they could let the emperor know, such as chanting for the end of a war. Regardless of whether these chants had any influence on the emperor, the Colosseum offered a political outlet for people who had little say in government.[91]

The Colosseum was also a place where Romans could receive gifts from the emperor. Traditionally, wealthy Romans gave gifts to the people as a social obligation, but it was politically advantageous for their careers as well. Since Romans flocked to the amphitheater for the games, it was a logical place for the emperor to dole out gifts to the people. Cassius Dio wrote that the emperor Titus "[t]hrew down into the Colosseum from aloft little wooden balls variously inscribed, one designating some article of food … or again horses, pack animals, cattle or slaves. Those who seized them were to carry them to the dispensers of the bounty, from whom they would receive the article named."[92] Food, especially meat, was most commonly distributed as a gift, and some ancient sources hint that the meat doled out to the people may have come from the animals killed in the arena. Wherever the meat came from, Romans greatly appreciated any gift, so it was a good way for the emperor to endear himself to the people.[93]

---

[90] Hopkins & Beard (2005) pp.50-55.
[91] Hopkins & Beard (2005) p.40.
[92] Cassius Dio, 66.25.4-5, in Kyle (1998) p.191.
[93] Kyle (1998) pp. 190-194 & Hopkins & Beard (2005) p.41.

The Colosseum after the Roman Empire

When the emperor Constantine converted to Christianity at the beginning of the 4th century, he enacted legislation against gladiatorial shows. In 325 A.D., for example, Constantine decreed, "In times in which peace and peace relating to domestic affairs prevail bloody demonstrations displease us. Therefore, we order that there may be no more gladiator combats. Those who were condemned to become gladiators for their crimes are to work from now on in the mines. Thus they pay for their crimes without having to pour their blood." In reality, Constantine mostly discouraged the spectacles in the amphitheatre rather than place an outright ban on them, so the Colosseum continued to act as a venue for the Roman spectacles for some time afterwards. The last recorded gladiatorial games held in the Colosseum occurred in the mid 430's, but in 523 a Roman senator named Cassiodorus recorded that the Gothic King Theodoric sponsored an animal show in the Colosseum. Despite religious and legislative opposition to these pagan spectacles, the Colosseum continued to function as intended by the Flavians well into the sixth century, likely due to their popularity.[94]

While the games continued, spectacles held within the Colosseum after Constantine became emperor were likely infrequent. Continual wars and invasions meant the Roman elite had limited funds to spend on shows for the people; in order to organize a successful show, enough money was needed to procure animals, gladiators and other attendants. Furthermore, by the 6th century, time, weather and natural disasters (including lightning strikes) were beginning to take their toll on the Colosseum, and once Constantine moved his capital to Constantinople in the early 4th century, the funding and infrastructure needed to maintain hundreds of structures within Rome were severely lacking. If the Roman elite did not have sufficient funds to sponsor spectacles, they assuredly would have spent very little to help restore the crumbling parts of the Flavian amphitheatre. Any patching that was done was likely cosmetic rather than permanent, and it is even probable that parts of the Colosseum were already being quarried for stone by the end of the 6th century.[95]

From the 6th century onwards, there is evidence that squatting within the Colosseum became more and more frequent. Housing began to appear in the amphitheatre, as well as animals, gardens, shacks, stalls, troughs and haylofts. One of the main functions of the Colosseum was now providing residence for blacksmiths, brick layers, lime-pit workers and many others. Over time, parts of the amphitheatre, such as the arena substructure, began to be buried as the Flavian amphitheatre became a medieval settlement.

Not every occupant was from the lower class. By 1150, about 13 arches on two levels at the eastern side of the Colosseum were incorporated into the "Frangipane Palace", owned by the Frangipane family. Frangipane was one of the dominant warlords in Rome at the time, and although the residence was called a palace it was probably more accurately a fortress. It remained in the hands of this family until around the end of the 13th century, when the "palace" was taken over by the Annibaldi family. By this time, the original function of the Colosseum had been forgotten, and guidebooks from the period frequently identified the ancient structure as an old temple dedicated to a Sun god or some other pagan deity. Regardless of the incorrect identification, there was still enough space within the Colosseum to accommodate a bullfight in 1332. Thus, at least for a brief moment, the Flavian amphitheatre once again held a spectacle within its crumbling walls.[96]

---

[94] Hopkins & Beard (2005) pp.152-153.
[95] Hopkins & Beard (2005) p.154.
[96] Hopkins & Beard (2005) pp.162-163 & Bomgardner (2000) p.30.

By the end of the 14th century the Colosseum was primarily controlled by the Church, and from 1490 to the middle of the 16th century a Passion play was held in the arena, harkening back to the reenacted myths once performed as a part of some executions. Although the Church seemingly had an interest in incorporating the Colosseum into Christian ritual, such as constructing a small chapel in 1519, they also continued to allow people to rob the stones. This had been occurring as far back as the 6th century, but it was during this period that the removal of bricks, stone and marble intensified. Some of the marble was taken to create lime, while cartloads of rubble were hauled off to create walls, palaces and churches, even including portions of the Vatican.[97]

When Renaissance scholars began reading the classical texts, they rediscovered the original function of the Colosseum as well, and the Colosseum was subsequently viewed as a monument of Christian importance, a place where early Christians were martyred. Many ancient accounts of Christians dying in "the amphitheatre" led to the belief that some were executed in the Colosseum, even though there is no evidence specifically mentioning Christians dying within the Flavian amphitheatre. Regardless of this change of status, quarrying continued, and some church figures, such as Pope Sixtus V, had interesting plans for the Colosseum. This included converting the Colosseum into a wool factory, with housing for the workers located on the second floor. Another idea proposed tearing down the amphitheatre so a road could be constructed. Fortunately, neither of these ideas materialized, but in 1594 some of the rooms on the lower floor were rented out to a glue factory.[98]

By the 17th century, the Colosseum continued to house a variety of businesses and local inhabitants, despite the recognition and belief that the amphitheatre was an important Christian monument. In the 1670's, the Church planned to construct another chapel within its walls, but a large wooden cross was constructed instead. Despite its religious significance, in 1700 the northern corridors of the amphitheatre became a manure dump for the manufacture of saltpeter. Finally, in 1749 the Catholic Church decreed that the Colosseum was sacred ground and dedicated the arena to the Passions of Christ by setting up Stations of the Cross. The next year, as a means to demonstrate Christian victory over paganism, Pope Benedict XIV erected a plaque celebrating the sacredness of the monument. It read:

> "The Flavian amphitheatre, famous for its triumphs and spectacles, dedicated to the gods of the pagans in the impious cult, redeemed by the blood of the martyrs from foul superstition. In order that the memory of their courage is not lost, Pope Benedict XIV, in the jubilee of 1750, the tenth year of his pontificate had rendered in stone the inscription painted on the walls by Pope Clement X in the jubilee of 1675, but faded through the ravages of time."[99]

---

[97] Hopkins & Beard (2005) p.167.
[98] Hopkins & Beard (2005) p.157.
[99] Hopkins & Beard (2005) pp.164-165.

Thomas Cole's Interior of the Colosseum Rome depicts different Stages of the Cross.

Finally, in the mid-18th century, quarrying stone from the Colosseum was no longer allowed. Instead, debris was removed and patch work commenced in an effort to stop the deterioration of the Flavian amphitheatre. There was much reconstruction that took place around the structure in the 19th century, including the large buttress to reinforce the outer ring still seen today. It was also during this time that archaeological work began more intensively, particularly of the substructure. Earlier archaeological excavations had occurred in the 15th century, when the drainage systems were unearthed, but very little had been done since then, and flooding of the substructure had prevented it from being entirely uncovered. In spite of all the efforts made to maintain and understand the history of the Colosseum, its religious significance continued as the Christian monuments within remained.[100]

In the 1870's, the Colosseum became a state monument rather than a religious one. The substructures were uncovered once again, and although there was outcry from many Catholics, including the Pope, the religious structures were torn down. Over the years, layers of earth were gradually removed from the Flavian amphitheatre, and in the 1930's, Mussolini reconstructed parts of the Colosseum in order to hold rallies for his fascist government. This included installing a section of seats that are still present. For a short time during World War II, the Colosseum became a weapons depot for the military and a bomb shelter for Roman citizens.

After the war, the Colosseum became a major tourist attraction visited by millions of people each year. This has ensured that restorations continually occur, even as time, traffic and pollution all take their toll on the nearly 2,000 year old building. Nevertheless, the Colosseum continues to be a magnificent towering monument that symbolizes important parts of Rome's history across two millennia. It represented the power of the Flavian family, paid for from the spoils of Vespasian's victory over the Jews, but even after the Roman Empire fell, the Colosseum endured. Its function changed continuously over the centuries, and its stones were frequently quarried, but the Colosseum always awed those who saw it. With proper care, the Colosseum

---

[100] Hopkins & Beard (2005) pp.171-172.

will hopefully endure for another 2,000 years.[101]

Online Resources

Other books about ancient history by Charles River Editors

Other books about ancient Rome by Charles River Editors

Bibliography

Brittanniae, Brittany. "Ancient Roman Superstars: Charioteers." *Latin Language Blog*. Transparent Language, Inc., 28 Jan. 2014. Web. 25 July 2017. <http://blogs.transparent.com/latin/ancient-roman-super-stars-charioteers/>.

Cartwright, Mark. "Circus Maximus." *Ancient History Encyclopedia*. Ancient History Encyclopedia, Ltd., 12 June 2013. Web. 25 July 2017. <http://www.ancient.eu/Circus_Maximus/>.

Editors, A View on Cities. "Circus Maximus." *A View on Cities*. A View on Cities, LLC, 2017. Web. 25 July 2017. <http://www.aviewoncities.com/rome/circusmaximus.htm>.

Editors, University of Chicago. "Circus Maximus." *University of Chicago Website*. University of Chicago, 2001. Web. 25 July 2017. <http://penelope.uchicago.edu/~grout/encyclopaedia_romana/circusmaximus/circusmaximus.html>.

Editors, Seeing Spectacles. "FAMOUS CHARIOTEERS." *Seeing Spectacles*. WordPress, 2012. Web. 25 July 2017. <http://www.seeingspectacles.org/?page_id=500>.

Zarley, David. "The Fifteen Billion Dollar Athlete." *Vice Sports*. Vice, Inc., 23 Mar. 2015. Web. 25 July 2017. <https://sports.vice.com/en_us/article/nzpgaq/the-fifteen-billion-dollar-athlete>.

Norris, Shawn T. "GAIUS APPULEIUS DIOCLES: THE WORLD'S 1ST SPORTS BILLIONAIRE." *Rome Across Europe*. WordPress, 10 Dec. 2016. Web. 25 July 2017. <http://www.romeacrosseurope.com/?p=5888#sthash.1CgKrgRi.CYsmViQw.dpbs>.

Editors, Tribunes and Triumphs. "Circus Maximus." *Tribunes and Triumphs*. Siteseen, Ltd., 2017. Web. 25 July 2017. <http://www.tribunesandtriumphs.org/colosseum/circus-maximus.htm>.

Editors, Early Church History. "SCORPUS THE CHARIOTEER." *Early Church History*. Early Church History, Ltd., 2012. Web. 25 July 2017. <https://earlychurchhistory.org/entertainment/scorpus-the-charioteer/>.

Editors, BBC History. "'Timeline: the rise and fall of the Roman games'." *BBC History*. BBC, 26 Nov. 2015. Web. 25 July 2017. <http://www.thecolchesterarchaeologist.co.uk/?p=23016>.

Bagchi, Rob. "Six reasons chariot racing was the best spectator sport." *The Telegraph*. Telegraph Media Group, Ltd., 30 Aug. 2016. Web. 25 July 2017. <http://www.telegraph.co.uk/films/ben-hur/best-spectator-sport/>.

McManus, Barbara F. "THE CIRCUS: ROMAN CHARIOT RACING." *V Roma*. The College of New Rochelle, July 2003. Web. 25 July 2017. <http://www.vroma.org/~bmcmanus/circus.html>.

Editors, PBS. "Chariot Races." *PBS - The Roman Empire*. Devillier Donegan Enterprises, 2006. Web. 25 July 2017. <http://www.pbs.org/empires/romans/empire/chariot.html>.

Moore, Malcolm. "The legend of Romulus and Remus." *The Telegraph*. Telegraph Media Group, Ltd., 21 Nov. 2007. Web. 25 July 2017. <http://www.telegraph.co.uk/news/uknews/1570109/The-legend-of-Romulus-and-Remus.html>.

---

[101] Hopkins & Beard (2005) pp.172-177.

Trueman, C. N. "Romulus and Remus." *The History Learning Site*. The History Learning Site, Ltd., 16 Mar. 2015. Web. 26 July 2017. <http://www.historylearningsite.co.uk/ancient-rome/romulus-and-remus/>.

Chowdhury, Rohini. "The Sons of Mars." *Long Long Time Ago*. Penguin Books India, 2005. Web. 26 July 2017. <http://www.longlongtimeago.com/once-upon-a-time/myths/roman-myths/the-sons-of-mars/>.

Lutwyche, Jayne. "Ancient Rome's maidens – who were the Vestal Virgins?" *BBC Religion & Ethics*. BBC, 7 Sept. 2012. Web. 26 July 2017. <http://www.bbc.co.uk/religion/0/18490233>.

Walsh, P. G. "House of the Vestals." *University of Chicago Website*. University of Chicago, 2006. Web. 26 July 2017. <http://penelope.uchicago.edu/~grout/encyclopaedia_romana/romanforum/vestals.html>.

Editors, Rome Reborn. "Circus Maximus." *Rome Reborn*. University of Virginia, 2008. Web. 26 July 2017. <http://romereborn.frischerconsulting.com/ge/AS-003.html>.

Cavazzi, F. "The Roman Kings." *Roman Empire*. Roman Empire.Net, 7 Apr. 2012. Web. 26 July 2017. <http://www.roman-empire.net/kings/kings-index.html>.

Galbi, Douglas. "Sabine women win Pyrrhic peace for Roman men." *Purple Motes*. WordPress, 3 Jan. 2016. Web. 26 July 2017. <https://www.purplemotes.net/2016/01/03/sabine-women-roman-men/>.

Darling, David. "Romulus and Remus." *Internet Encyclopedia of History*. The Worlds of David Darling, 2017. Web. 26 July 2017. <http://www.daviddarling.info/encyclopedia_of_history/R/Romulus_and_Remus.html>.

Plubins, Rodrigo Quijada. "Chariot." *Ancient History Encyclopedia*. Ancient History Encyclopedia, Ltd., 6 Mar. 2013. Web. 27 July 2017. <http://www.ancient.eu/chariot/>.

Lorenzi, Rossella. "This Secret Feature Kept Ancient Roman Chariots From Crashing." *Seeker*. Seeker, Inc., 10 Jan. 2017. Web. 27 July 2017. <https://www.seeker.com/secret-of-roman-race-chariots-found-2187581176.html>.

Fagan, Garrett G., PhD. "Chariot Racing: Ancient Rome's Most Dangerous Sport." *The Great Courses Daily*. The Teaching Company, LLC, 2016. Web. 27 July 2017. <http://www.thegreatcoursesdaily.com/chariot-racing/>.

King, Carol. "The Romans: Chariot Racing." *Italy Magazine*. Bluespark, Ltd., 7 July 2014. Web. 27 July 2017. <http://www.italymagazine.com/featured-story/romans-chariot-racing>.

Editors, Rome Total War Heaven. "Chariot Racing." *Rome Total War Heaven*. HeavenGames, LLC, 2016. Web. 27 July 2017. <http://rtw.heavengames.com/history/general/chariot_racing/index.shtml>.

Cartwright, Mark. "Roman Games, Chariot Races & Spectacle." *Ancient History Encyclopedia*. Ancient History Encyclopedia, Ltd., 24 Dec. 2013. Web. 27 July 2017. <http://www.ancient.eu/article/635/>.

Gill, N. S. "The Roman King L. Tarquinius Priscus According to Livy." *Thought Company*. Thought Company, Inc., 9 Feb. 2017. Web. 27 July 2017. <https://www.thoughtco.com/l-tarquinius-priscus-112620>.

Editors, Biography Base. "Lucius Tarquinius Priscus Biography." *Biography Base*. Biography Base, LLC, 2014. Web. 27 July 2017. <http://www.biographybase.com/biography/Tarquinius_Priscus_Lucius.html>.

Norris, Shawn T. "LUCIUS TARQUINIUS PRISCUS: THE ELDER KING (#5)." *Rome Across Europe*. WordPress, 24 Sept. 2016. Web. 27 July 2017. <http://www.romeacrosseurope.com/?p=4788#sthash.haAOnZtP.Ohg3aDrR.dpbs>.

Editors, Ancient Origins. "Superweapon of the Ancient World: A History of Chariots - Part I." *Ancient Origins*. Novus Web Solutions, 18 June 2015. Web. 27 July 2017. <http://www.ancient-origins.net/artifacts-ancient-technology/superweapon-ancient-world-history-chariots-part-i-003254>.

Editors, Antiquity Now. "KIDS' BLOG! The Invention of the Wheel: How the Ancient Sumerians Got Humanity Rollin'!" *Antiquity Now*. WordPress, 20 Aug. 2013. Web. 27 July 2017. <https://antiquitynow.org/2013/08/20/kids-blog-the-invention-of-the-wheel-how-the-ancient-sumerians-got-humanity-rollin/>.

Editors, Khan Academy. "Standard of Ur and other objects from the Royal Graves." *Khan Academy*. Khan Academy Organization, 2014. Web. 27 July 2017. <https://www.khanacademy.org/humanities/ancient-art-civilizations/ancient-near-east1/sumerian/a/standard-of-ur-and-other-objects-from-the-royal-graves>.

Wishart, Michelle. "History of Archery Bows." *AZ Central*. AZ Central, LLC, 2013. Web. 27 July 2017. <http://healthyliving.azcentral.com/history-archery-bows-5909.html>.

Editors, HistoryNet. " Battle of Kadesh." *HistoryNet*. World History Group, 31 July 2006. Web. 27 July 2017. <http://www.historynet.com/battle-of-kadesh.htm>.

Editors, Oxford Reference. "Lucius Tarquinius Priscus." *Oxford Reference*. Oxford University Press, 2015. Web. 27 July 2017. <http://www.oxfordreference.com/view/10.1093/oi/authority.20110803102143242>.

Editors, Cosa Visitare a Roma. "Circus Maximus (Circo Massimo)." *Cosa Visitare a Roma*. Cosa Visitare a Roma, LLC, 2014. Web. 27 July 2017. <http://www.cosavisitarearoma.it/circus-maximus.html>.

Gill, N. S. "What Was the Roman Circus Maximus?" *Thought Company*. Thought Company, Inc., 10 Feb. 2017. Web. 27 July 2017. <https://www.thoughtco.com/the-circus-maximus-and-the-roman-circus-117832>.

Editors, Maria MIlani. "Circus Maximus." *Maria MIlani*. Maria MIlani, Ltd., 2014. Web. 28 July 2017. <http://www.mariamilani.com/ancient_rome/circus_maximus.htm>.

Shackleton-Bailey, D. R. "The Elephant in Rome." *University of Chicago Website*. University of Chicago, 2001. Web. 28 July 2017. <http://penelope.uchicago.edu/~grout/encyclopaedia_romana/gladiators/elephantus.html>.

Beall, Abigail. "Welcome to Ben Hur's shopping mall: Scientists uncover launderettes, bars, brothels and betting shops at scene of famous Roman chariot race." *Daily Mail*. Associated Newspapers, Ltd., 17 Nov. 2016. Web. 28 July 2017. <http://www.dailymail.co.uk/sciencetech/article-3942694/Ancient-latrines-lucky-horse-New-finds-Circus-Maximus.html>.

Editors, Rome Reborn. "Circus Maximus." *Rome Reborn*. University of Virginia, 2008. Web. 28 July 2017. <http://archive1.village.virginia.edu/spw4s/RomanForum/GoogleEarth/AK_GE/AK_HTML/AS-003.html>.

Editors, History Channel. "Pawning Through the Ages." *History Channel*. A&E Television Networks, LLC, 2016. Web. 28 July 2017. <http://www.history.com/shows/pawn-stars/articles/pawning-through-the-ages>.

Editors, Revealed Rome. "HIDDEN BENEATH CIRCUS MAXIMUS, AN UNDERGROUND — AND SECRET — MITHRAIC TEMPLE." *Revealed Rome*. Revealed Rome, Ltd., 21 Feb. 2011. Web. 28 July 2017.

<http://www.revealedrome.com/2011/02/underground-circus-maximus-mithraic-cult-mithras-mithraeum-rome-subterranean.html>.

Murdock, D. M., and Acharya S. "Mithra: The Pagan Christ." *Acharya S' Truth Be Known*. Stellar House Publishing, July 2017. Web. 28 July 2017. <http://www.truthbeknown.com/mithra.htm>.

Lawrence, Caroline. "Fun Chariot Facts." *Roman Mysteries & Western Mysteries*. Blogspot, 15 Jan. 2010. Web. 28 July 2017. <http://flavias.blogspot.tw/2010/01/fun-chariot-facts.html>.

Editors, Sights of Rome. "The Circus Maximus." *Sights of Rome*. Blogspot, 4 July 2013. Web. 28 July 2017. <http://sightsofrome.blogspot.tw/2013/07/the-circus-maximus.html>.

Editors, Ancient Peoples. "Roman Chariot Teams and Their Sport." *Ancient Peoples*. Tumblr, Inc., 24 Apr. 2015. Web. 28 July 2017. <https://ancientpeoples.tumblr.com/post/48772948462/roman-chariot-teams-and-their-sport-introduction>.

Editors, Trevor Bloom. "How dangerous was Roman chariot-racing?" *Trevor Bloom*. Trevor Bloom, Mar. 2011. Web. 28 July 2017. <http://www.trevorbloom.com/2011/03/how-dangerous-was-roman-chariot-racing/>.

Ashby, Carol. "CHARIOT RACING." *Carol Ashby Official Website*. WordPress, 2016. Web. 28 July 2017. <https://carolashby.com/chariot-racing/>.

Editors, The One and the Many: Devoted to the Universal and the Particulars. "Ancient Roman Prayer." *The One and the Many: Devoted to the Universal and the Particulars*. WordPress, 18 Feb. 2008. Web. 28 July 2017. <https://universalparticulars.wordpress.com/2008/02/18/ancient-roman-prayer/>.

Sheldon, Natasha. "Ludi Romani Festival: Roman Religious Games." *Decoded Past*. WordPress, 5 Sept. 2014. Web. 28 July 2017. <http://decodedpast.com/ludi-romani-festival-roman-religious-games/13319>.

Editors, The Colchester Archaeologist. "Roman festival of Cerealia at the Circus Maximus." *The Colchester Archaeologist*. The Colchester Archaeologist, Ltd., 12 Apr. 2016. Web. 28 July 2017. <http://www.thecolchesterarchaeologist.co.uk/?p=26227>.

Editors, Revolvy. " Ludi scaenici ." *Revolvy*. Revolvy, LLC, 1 June 2017. Web. 28 July 2017. <https://www.revolvy.com/main/index.php?s=Ludi%20scaenici&item_type=topic>.

Editors, Early Church History. "BOXING IN THE ANCIENT ROMAN WORLD." *Early Church History*. Early Church History, Ltd., 2013. Web. 28 July 2017. <https://earlychurchhistory.org/entertainment/boxing-in-ancient-roman-world/>.

Ravilious, Kate. " Gladiators Played by the Rules, Skulls Suggest." *National Geographic News*. National Geographic Partners, LLC, 3 Mar. 2006. Web. 28 July 2017. <http://news.nationalgeographic.com/news/2006/03/0303_060303_gladiators.html>.

Andrews, Evan. "10 Things You May Not Know About Roman Gladiators." *History Lists*. A&E Television Networks, LLC, 4 Mar. 2014. Web. 28 July 2017. <http://www.history.com/news/history-lists/10-things-you-may-not-know-about-roman-gladiators>.

Editors, My Extended Roman Holiday. "Ovid on picking up a girl at the Circus Maximus from his Ars Amatoria (Art of Love)." *My Extended Roman Holiday*. Blogspot, 27 May 2009. Web. 28 July 2017. <http://samsromanholiday.blogspot.tw/2009/05/ovid-on-picking-up-girl-at-circus.html>.

Editors, Rome Reborn. "Augustan Obelisk from the Circus Maximus." *Rome Reborn*. University of Virginia, 2008. Web. 28 July 2017.

<http://archive1.village.virginia.edu/spw4s/RomanForum/GoogleEarth/AK_GE/AK_HTML/OB-002.html>.

Stutowski, Dariusz. "Emperor Nero Competed in The Olympics' Chariot racing With 6 Horses More Than His Competitors." *History Collection*. Spike Media, Inc., Apr. 2017. Web. 28 July 2017. <http://historycollection.co/nero-olympic-hero/2/>.

Editors, PBS. "The Great Fire of Rome." *PBS - Secrets of the Dead*. Thirteen Productions, LLC, 2015. Web. 28 July 2017. <http://www.pbs.org/wnet/secrets/great-fire-rome-background/1446/>.

Thayer, Bill. "The Life of Probus." *University of Chicago Website*. University of Chicago, 2011. Web. 28 July 2017. <http://penelope.uchicago.edu/Thayer/e/roman/texts/historia_augusta/probus*.html>.

Plutarch. *Delphi Complete Works of Plutarch (Illustrated)*. 1st ed. Vol. 13. N.p.: n.p., 2013. Print. Delphi Ancient Classics.

Murphy, Trevor. *Pliny the Elder's Natural History: The Empire in the Encyclopedia*. 1st ed. N.p.: Oxford U Press, 2004. Print.

Free Books by Charles River Editors

We have brand new titles available for free most days of the week. To see which of our titles are currently free, click on this link.

Discounted Books by Charles River Editors
We have titles at a discount price of just 99 cents everyday. To see which of our titles are currently 99 cents, click on this link.

Printed in Great Britain
by Amazon